HISTORY OF
THE REDEEMED CHRISTIAN CHURCH OF GOD
IN ATLANTIC CANADA

A Tale of Enduring Faith

COMPILED BY
TUNDE APANTAKU, MD & PASTOR GBENGA ADENUGA
FOREWORD BY
PASTOR FEMI OLAWALE, PH.D.
Continental Overseer, RCCG Americas Continent II

History of RCCG in Atlantic Canada: A Tale of Enduring Faith.

Copyright © 2024 by Tunde Apantaku.

All rights reserved. No part of this publication may be reproduced, distributed or transmitted in any form or by any means, including photocopying, recording, or other electronic or mechanical methods, without the prior written permission of the publisher, except in the case of brief quotations embodied in critical reviews and certain other non-commercial uses permitted by copyright law.

Unless otherwise noted, Scripture quotations are from the New King James Version, copyright © 1982 by Thomas Nelson, Inc.

Permissions: Email publication@rccgatlantic.church, Attn: Tunde Apantaku.

Quantity Sales: Special discounts are available on quantity purchases by corporations, associations, churches, and denominations. For details, email publication@rccgatlantic.church, Attn: Special Sales Department.

Paperback ISBN: 978-1-0688491-3-8
Hardback ISBN: 978-1-0688491-1-4

Published By

The Publishing Pad
www.thepublishingpad.com

Dedication

For all early-days Christian missionaries, those who brought the good news to Africa. Thank you for enduring the hardship and adversity of the continent.

We are blessed by the faith of our founder, Pa Josiah Olufemi Akindayomi (1909–1980), and our General Overseer, Pastor Enoch Adejare Adeboye, whom God used in ways most of us may never fully get to know as they stood their grounds to guard and guide the foundational truth over the generations.

And most of all, for our Lord and Saviour, Jesus Christ, from whom all blessings flow.

Praise God the Father, Son, and Holy Ghost!

Contents

Foreword: When the Fullness of Time Came 1

Editor's Note 3

1   History of RCCG: How It All Started 5

2   RCCG in North America 17

3   RCCG in Atlantic Canada 21

4   Our Leaders Along the Journey 33

5   Growth of RCCG in Atlantic Canada 47

6   Our Statement of Faith 87

7   RCCG Atlantic Canada Conference Profile 97

About the Compilers 119

FOREWORD

When the Fullness of Time Came
by
Pastor Femi Olawale

To everything under the sun there is a season and a time. Every good work is birthed by a vision, and the vision is for an appointed time. The vision for the Atlantic Canada Mission field was inspired by the Canadian official motto carried on its coat of arms, *A Mari Usque ad Mare*, which means "From Sea to Sea." It is a direct quote from Psalm 72:8, "He shall have dominion from sea to sea, and from the river to the ends of the earth." If Canada sought dominion from sea to sea, how much more should our mission field traverse across seas!

There was no church in Atlantic Canada. We had gone to British Columbia, and Calgary, Alberta, but nothing in the Atlantic. We were trusting God for an open door. I was the Zonal Coordinator for Zone 17 RCCGNA and the Mission Administrator for Canada.

Years passed. The breakthrough came in 2006 when Pastor Tayo Ojajuni, now an Assistant Continental Overseer, forwarded me a request from Nigeria: Provincial Pastor Sola Balogun of Lagos Province 15 had a missionary interested in coming to Canada. In collaboration with Canada Mission, the first church in the Atlantic region—Jesus House Halifax in Nova Scotia—was pioneered in 2007 by the missionary, Pastor Gladys Omamofe, now a Zonal Coordinator.

The next field was Cornerstone Chapel Moncton, in the province of New Brunswick, pioneered by Pastors Gbenga and Bisi Adenuga, now Provincial Pastors of Atlantic Canada. Prince Edward Island (PEI) was the next port of call. Omega Parish metamorphosed over the years into Living Word Assembly. Then, back to Halifax, Restoration Chapel

Halifax was next, pioneered by Pastors Simeon and Juliet Fagbile, now Zonal Coordinators. The rest is now history! We had secured the Atlantic region. We had achieved "coast to coast"—from Vancouver, British Columbia, to St. John's, Newfoundland. We then began to expand in all the cardinal directions in every province until this day!

It is now seventeen years after, and Atlantic Canada has sixteen parishes and still counting. The expansion is satisfactory even as there is room for improvement. There is a divine call to do much more. We keep moving. To God alone be all the glory, in Jesus' name.

Pastor Femi Olawale, PhD
Continental Overseer—RCCG Americas Continent II

Editor's Note

The Apostle Paul wrote,

> *Do not lose heart. [. . .] For our light affliction, which is but for a moment, is working for us a far more exceeding and eternal weight of glory, while we do not look at the things which are seen, but at the things which are not seen.*
> —II Corinthians 4:16a–18a

Perseverance, or enduring faith, simply put, may be defined as possessing a forward-looking perspective and searching against all odds. It is the steadfast pursuit of a goal or objective despite facing obstacles, challenges, setbacks, or failures. It involves maintaining determination, resilience, and persistence in the face of adversity. Therefore, it is an essential quality for achieving long-term success in various aspects of life, including personal, academic, professional, and creative endeavours. In the context of Christian belief, perseverance involves enduring hardships, staying true to one's conviction, and continuing to grow spiritually despite challenges. Accordingly, it requires relying on God's strength and guidance to overcome obstacles and remain steadfast in living out one's faith.

As such, perseverance is often fueled by a strong belief in God's abilities, a clear vision of your desired outcome, and a willingness to continue striving even when circumstances are difficult.

Where opposition abounds, you are encouraged to realize that God planned it, and it will turn out for good.

When challenges get tough, you must be reassured that God allowed it, and it will turn out for the better.

When afflictions arise, you should be joyful that God is always in control, and it will turn out for the best.

Of note, perseverance is not just about enduring difficulties but also about learning from experiences, adapting, and continuing to move forward despite the odds.

As you read through this book, *History of RCCG in Atlantic Canada: A Tale of Enduring Faith,* you will learn of single-minded men and women of faith as they tell their stories—how they looked beyond immediate hardship and how God came through for them—in their own words. One thing that is common in all their stories is that each of these men and women saw God use their hard times to create for Himself something glorious.

As you read this book, we hope the Spirit of God will help you meditate rightly on a simple but deep question: Can I see God's purpose in enduring my difficult circumstances?

Pastor Dr. Tunde Apantaku, MD, FRCPC, MA (Min.)

CHAPTER ONE

History of RCCG: How It All Started

Arise, shine;
For your light has come!
And the glory of the Lord is risen upon you.
For behold, the darkness shall cover the earth,
And deep darkness the people;
But the Lord will arise over you,
And His glory will be seen upon you.
The Gentiles shall come to your light,
And kings to the brightness of your rising.
—Isaiah 60:1–3

PA JOSIAH AKINDAYOMI

In July 1909, baby boy Josiah was born into the Akindayomi family of Ondo State in Nigeria. Even though this child grew up surrounded by idol worshippers, he knew there existed a greater power, and he yearned to know "the God who created the Earth and everyone on it." This pursuit for God led him to the Church Missionary Society (CMS), where he was baptized in 1927. Still spiritually unfulfilled, he joined the Cherubim and Seraphim (C&S) church in 1931. Whilst there, he began to hear a voice within him saying, "You will be my servant." Since this was not his intention, he decided to ignore the voice. This went on for seven years, during which all the business ventures he tried resulted in failure. In debt and without peace of mind, he found himself totally dependent on the grace of God. Here marked the beginning of a definite relationship with God. Totally broken, he yielded, saying, "Lord, I will go wherever you want me to go." He asked for signs to confirm that this was indeed God's call. The confirmation came through the Bible passages of Jeremiah 1:4–10, Isaiah 41:10–13, and Romans 8:29–31. The Lord assured him that He would provide for all his needs, as he would not receive any salary from that point on. This proved to be a comforting reminder during the trials in the months ahead.

In 1947, Pa Josiah Akindayomi started to become concerned that the Cherubim and Seraphim (C&S) church movement was departing from the true Word of God in some of its practices. By 1952, he felt totally persuaded to leave the Cherubim and Seraphim (C&S) church. He started a house fellowship, called the Glory of God Fellowship, at Willoughby Street, Ebute-Metta, Lagos. Initially there were nine members, but before long, the fellowship rapidly grew as news spread of the miracles that occurred in their midst. Akindayomi later had a vision of words that appeared to be written on a blackboard. The words were *The Redeemed Christian Church of God.* Amazingly, Pa Akindayomi, who could not read or write, was supernaturally able to write these words down. In this visitation, God also said to him that this church would go to the ends of the Earth and that when the Lord Jesus Christ appeared in glory, He would meet the church. The Lord then established a covenant with Pa Akindayomi, analogous to the Abrahamic covenant in the Bible. He said that He the Lord would meet all the needs of the church in an awesome way if only members would serve Him faithfully and be obedient to His Word. It is upon this covenant that the Redeemed Christian Church of God was built.

The Redeemed Christian Church of God (RCCG) was born in 1952, destined by the Lord Himself to take the world for Him. The church continued to meet at 9 Willoughby Street until they were able to acquire some land, thereby witnessing a relocation to the present site of the headquarters of the church at 1–5 Redemption Way, Ebute-Metta, Lagos, Nigeria (formerly 1a, Cemetery Street).

Sometime in the early 1970s, God had spoken to Pa Akindayomi about his successor. The Lord told him that this man, who was not a member of the church then, would be a young, educated man. Consequently, when a young university lecturer joined the church in 1973, Papa was able to recognize him in the Spirit as the one the Lord had spoken about in the past. This man, Enoch Adejare Adeboye, who was then a lecturer of mathematics at the University of Lagos, soon became involved in the church. He became one of the interpreters translating Pa Akindayomi's sermons from Yoruba to English. He was ordained a pastor of RCCG in 1975.

In 1980, Pa Josiah Akindayomi died at seventy-one years of age. While Papa was preparing to meet his Creator, he sent for Pastor Enoch Adeboye and spent several hours sharing with him details of the covenant and the plans of the Lord for the church. Even though, a year before this, the Lord had revealed to Pastor Adeboye that he would be Papa's successor, it was still too difficult for him to fully contemplate such an awesome responsibility. Amidst controversy, Pastor Adeboye's appointment was formalized by the reading of Pa Akindayomi's sealed pronouncement after his burial. Pastor Adeboye succeeded Pa Akindayomi on November 22, 1980.

In 1981, an open explosion began, and the number of parishes has since grown by leaps and bounds. At last count, there were at least 2,000 parishes of the Redeemed Christian Church of God in Nigeria. On the international scene, the church is present in other African nations, including Côte D'Ivoire, Ghana, Zambia, Malawi, Zaire, Tanzania, Kenya, Uganda, Gambia, Cameroon, and South Africa. In Europe, the church is fully established in the United Kingdom, Netherlands, Spain, Italy, Germany, Greece, France, Switzerland, Austria, Denmark, Sweden, and Norway. In North America, over 1,654 parishes are spread across various cities in the USA and Canada. Also, there are parishes in the Caribbean countries of Haiti and Jamaica. There are parishes in South America, the Middle East, and Australia as well.

Today, God is still doing marvelous deeds worldwide through The Redeemed Christian Church of God. One of the well-known programs of the church is the Holy Ghost Service, an all-night miracle service that is held on the first Friday of every month at the Redemption Camp at Km. 46, Lagos–Ibadan Expressway. The average head count of those who attend the Service is in the millions. The Holy Ghost Service is now held all around the world and is led by Pastor E.A. Adeboye, half-yearly in London, UK. Similarly, Pastor E.A. Adeboye leads these services in Washington, DC, and Toronto, Ontario, once a year, and once every other year in mainland Europe.

PASTOR ENOCH ADEJARE ADEBOYE (Daddy G.O.)

Pastor Enoch Adejare Adeboye (popularly known as Daddy G.O.) was born on March 2, 1942, into a humble family in the village of Ifewara, Osun State, located in the southwestern part of Nigeria. His poor family background seemed at first glance capable of confining him to a life of lack. Brilliant, calm, and reticent, the lad had a scholarly aura, and his early teachers had little doubt that he was cut out for academia. The bruising truth was that Enoch's tall ambition to pursue a career in academia was irreconcilable with the abject poverty of his family. Not to be deterred, his parents sold a few cherished possessions and borrowed from kind neighbours just to ensure that their son's dream was not held back.

In 1956, Enoch was admitted into one of Nigeria's foremost secondary schools, Ilesha Grammar School, Osun State. As a youth, he discovered a passion for books and an aptitude for science and, in particular, mathematics. This led him to pursue higher education in the same field. He obtained a bachelor's degree in mathematics from the University of Ife, Nigeria, in 1967, a master's degree in hydrodynamics from the University of Lagos, Nigeria, in 1969, and a doctorate in applied mathematics from the same university in 1975. He had planned to become the youngest university president (vice-chancellor) in Africa.

On July 29, 1973, Enoch Adeboye made a personal commitment to Christ through the ministry of Reverend Josiah Olufemi Akindayomi, the founder and first general overseer of The Redeemed Christian Church of God. Ordained a pastor in RCCG in 1977, Pastor Adeboye received a solid foundation in the scriptures and, unbeknownst to him, was being groomed for the future assignment under the tutelage of Reverend Akindayomi.

In 1981, when the founder passed to glory, the baton of leadership was handed over to Pastor Adeboye by divine orchestration. His appointment as General Overseer immediately terminated his academic career, and as a result, he set his heart on taking RCCG to the next level of ministry, where all strata of society could be involved in the ministry without compromising the true worship of God.

Since 1981, under his leadership, RCCG has grown in size and now has parishes in about 198 countries, including over 300 in Canada. As of March 2024, there are sixteen parishes in Atlantic Canada, and RCCG is considered by many in the faith community to be the fastest-growing Christian denomination in the world.

Pastor E.A. Adeboye organizes monthly Holy Ghost services in Nigeria, with millions attending at the Redemption Camp's arena, which covers three square kilometres on the outskirts of Lagos. He also presides over the RCCG Convention in August and the RCCG Congress in December of each year.

Pastor E.A. Adeboye has endowed four Nigerian universities and received several honorary doctorates, including Doctor of Theology in 2009 from Canada Christian College and Doctor of Divinity from Oral Roberts University in 2022. Other relevant awards and recognitions include:

1999: Received honorary citizenship and a key to the city of Cambridge, Massachusetts, USA.
2000: Dedicated the first chapel in the Nigerian presidential villa in Abuja, Nigeria.
2002: Received a key to the city of Detroit, Michigan.
2005: Received honorary citizenship and a key to the city of Dallas, Texas, USA.
2005: Received honorary citizenship and a key to the city of Baltimore, Maryland, USA.
2008: Was awarded a National Honour (Order of the Federal Republic of Nigeria).

2009: Led the pre-summit prayers at the 64th General Assembly of the United Nations in New York.
2010: Was awarded a national sports honour (Spiritual Pillar of Nigerian Sports).
2011: Received award as the Best/Most Profitable Icon/Personality in Nigeria.
2014: Was awarded a National Honour (Commander of the Order of the Niger).
2015: Received a certificate of recognition from the Congress of the United States of America.

The highlights of Pastor E.A. Adeboye's ongoing ministry include:

- The monthly Holy Ghost Service (HGS), an open-air meeting in Nigeria with an average attendance of over one million people.
- The annual March three-day Special Holy Ghost Service (SHGS), an open-air meeting in Nigeria with an average attendance of over six million people.
- The annual December weeklong Holy Ghost Congress (HGC), an open-air meeting in Nigeria with an average attendance of over twelve million people.
- The quarterly Festival of Life, an indoor revival meeting in London, UK, with an average attendance of over 50,000 people.
- The annual RCCG conventions in Nigeria, UK, Asia, and the US/Canada, with an average attendance of over seven million (Nigeria), 50,000 (UK), and 10,000 (US/Canada).
- Television programs broadcast on a digital cable channel called Open Heavens TV as well as on Liveway TV and satellite radio.
- Author of over sixty books. His daily devotional manual, *Open Heavens*, is globally distributed and widely read, with over one million copies printed annually in English, French, and other major languages of the world.

Pastor E.A. Adeboye has unrestricted access to many world leaders and was the only clergy named amongst the *50 Most Powerful People in the World* by *Newsweek* Magazine (USA) in December 2008. More recently, in 2019, he was named one of the top 100 most influential Africans by *New African* magazine. Pastor Adeboye has been married to Folu Adeboye since 17 December 1967, and he has four children and several grandchildren. Many biographies and films have depicted his life. The latest such effort—*Enoch*, a biographical film written and directed by Damilola Mike-Bamiloye—debuted in May 2023.

PASTOR MRS. FOLU ADEBOYE (Mummy G.O.)

Foluke Adenike Adeboye (née Adeyokunnu), born 13 July 1948, is a seasoned educator, philanthropist, administrator, counsellor, mentor, and pastor with over forty years of professional experience as an educational advisor, administrator, and teacher. She provides congregational leadership and pastoral care and engages in missionary support work, particularly with women and children. With a passion for quality education, she has made immense contributions to the education sector in Africa as the founder of a vigorous educational movement known as Christ the Redeemer's Schools Movement, which has led to the founding of over twenty quality Christian educational institutions caring for the educational welfare of children in Nigeria and across Africa.

Pastor Mrs. Folu Adeboye provides strategic leadership oversight to the teens' and children's education programs, working with the education board to update the curriculum, the teaching process, and policies and to ensure that proper educational ethics, compliance, and training are followed. She has been the chairperson of Christ the Redeemer's Ministries (CRM) School Movement since 1990, providing strategic vison and direction for the structure of education in the Redeemed Christian Church of God school system with educational policies that promote leading-edge, best-in-class educational excellence. She also provides strategic advisory oversight to ensure RCCG schools adopt a unified vision and mission and good governance and management systems, which promote accountability, high ethics, and good fiscal practices.

Apart from her influence in education, Pastor Mrs. Folu has, to her credit, founded or championed several charities, including Africa Missions Global, Habitation of Hope, Wholistic Outreach, Friends of Jesus, and CADAM, to mention a few. She is the Visionaire and Founder of Africa Missions Global (AMG), a faith-based not-for-profit NGO she founded in July 1996 to rescue and empower humanity through its charitable causes of providing education, water, health care, and empowerment initiatives. Through her passion for education, AMG has ten schools under its umbrella in five African countries. Some of the schools provide food for the children in keeping with the UN's Sustainable Development Goals of quality education and zero hunger. Her charitable achievements have touched education, health care, water provision, empowerment, emergency response, shelter, and the general welfare of underprivileged people, mostly in rural communities.

One of the educational projects under the umbrella of the charity Africa Missions Global is the Redeemer's Basic Boarding School, Koma Hills, Adamawa State, Nigeria—a total boarding primary and secondary school in the hilly region of northeast Nigeria. When Mrs. Adeboye intervened in this rural community in the late 1990s, they were far removed from society and wore no clothes. Today, through the school in Koma Hills, this community is now well known, with children from the school coming in tops in educational achievements in Adamawa State. The school is equipped with classroom blocks, hostels, libraries, dining facilities, boreholes, and solar energy for the provision of clean energy. There are several other education initiatives across Nigeria, Lesotho, Sierra Leone, Djibouti, Chad, and elsewhere.

Pastor F. Adeboye directs several other Corporate Social Responsibility (CSR) projects:

The Africa Missions Water for Life project aims at providing potable water for remote target locations in Africa.

Global Habitation of Hope Charity provides primary health care and eyeglasses, and in some cases, it has facilitated the provision or building of health centres in rural African communities.

The Wholistic Ministry aims to contribute to ending poverty through its empowerment initiatives by encouraging individuals and communities to take control of their lives and reduce their dependence on hand-outs and aid. Through the Wholistic Ministry, vulnerable women are empowered. Africa Missions Global has built vocational training centers across Africa and also provided a hub for the beneficiaries to carry out their business in one of the locations. At the height of the crisis in Sudan, Africa Missions facilitated the provision of a vocational centre for Sudanese widows who were refugees in Egypt.

The Wholistic Ministry also offers integrated shelters for vulnerable girls and women. The Wholistic Outreach, a faith-based non-profit initiative, was founded in April 2002 by Pastor Mrs. Folu Adeboye to offer social services and promote the development of youth and women, particularly vulnerable women. The vision is traceable to the moral decadence in society, reflected in the hordes of commercial sex workers and the increase in the numbers of pregnant and stranded teenagers, neglected young girls, and ladies in various stages of destitution, who are all suffering from the effects of this decadence. The organization is currently active and effective in the work of social reformation to give these girls and women the hope of a better life.

Relief supplies have been provided in response to crises posed by insurgency, terrorism, and epidemics, helping individuals and communities cope with the unfortunate consequences of such events. Worthy of note is the distribution of essential drugs, food, Ebola protection kits, and other relief materials during the 2010 Ebola crisis in the three worst-hit nations of Africa (Liberia, Sierra Leone, and Guinea Conakry). Internally displaced persons in Maiduguri, Abuja, and Yola, Nigeria, were provided with shelters and relief supplies as well as free education for their children.

Shelters and orphanages have been another important aspect of AMG's post-disaster response. Many shelter seekers had to take refuge far from their homes because alternative shelters were not available nearby. AMG provided equipped emergency shelters to give succour to many internally displaced persons in Northern Nigeria who lost their homes to insurgencies or terrorism and to children who became orphans as a result of such incidents. These shelters serve as temporary safe spaces where people can stabilize until they are able to return home.

Habitation of Hope is an integrated shelter for homeless and vulnerable boys between the ages of seven and eighteen. Pastor Mrs. Folu Adeboye founded the initiative in 2006 to rescue depressed and destitute boys from the streets and drug dens, transform and empower them, and give them the opportunity to develop into responsible citizens. The vision is to totally remove street children from the nation of Nigeria by helping these children reconcile with their families and settle back into their homes. It is an initiative set up to give hope to the hopeless.

Friends of Jesus is an initiative targeted at those who are less privileged and destitute in the immediate community of the Redemption Camp in Ogun State, Nigeria. It is focused on meeting their basic needs of food, shelter, and resettlement, as the case may be.

CADAM (Christ Against Drug Abuse Ministries), founded in 1991 by Pastor Ezekiel A. Odeyemi of Redeemed Christian Church of God, provides treatment and rehabilitation of drug addicts, both male and female. The initiative provides a one-year residential rehabilitation program. It started in rented premises only for men in Poka, Epe, Lagos State, Nigeria. In 2003, another facility was initiated to cater to women.

The Health Village is an inspirational and evolving health initiative founded in response to the health care challenges in the country of Nigeria. Pastor Mrs. F. Adeboye pioneered the project to build a health village in the environs of the Redemption Camp in Ogun State, Nigeria.

When actualized, this project will be one of the most comprehensive integrated health initiatives on the continent, providing a wide range of quality and affordable health services to anyone requiring such.

In pursuit of her goal of making specialist health care available in Nigeria, Pastor Mrs. F. Adeboye is a major co-sponsor, with her husband, Pastor E. A. Adeboye, of the many dialysis and intensive care units donated to university teaching hospitals across Nigeria through the His Love Foundation.

* * *

Pastor Mrs. Folu Adeboye is a conference speaker and has published widely, with many of her speeches transcribed into book form. She has also written the following books:

- *Kingdom Love* (2008)
- *Heaven in Your Home* (2006)
- *The Mother in Christ* (2004)
- *The Seven Secrets of Great Achievers* (2003)
- *This Also Shall Pass* (CRM, 2001)
- *Can I Cry Out?* (Oldavent Limited, 1999)
- *The Pastors' Wives Manual* (Feyisetan Press, 1995)
- *Divine Love*, a joint publication with her husband, Pastor E.A. Adeboye

In spite of her very loaded life, she finds time for recreation and has interest in counselling, mentoring, missions, church planting, children, healthy lifestyle, exercising, and walking.

CHAPTER TWO

RCCG in North America

Behold, I will do a new thing,
Now it shall spring forth;
Shall you not know it?
I will even make a road in the wilderness
And rivers in the desert.
—Isaiah 43:18–20

The Beginnings of RCCG in North America

The first RCCG parish in North America was Winner's Chapel in Detroit, Michigan. It was established on April 5, 1991, by James Fadel, an engineer with Ford Motor Company in Dearborn, Michigan. Fadel, who was mentored by Pastor E.A. Adeboye, the general overseer of RCCG Worldwide, had come to the United States for an academic program. He started a small fellowship with other migrants in his house, and it was this fellowship that metamorphosed into the RCCG Winner's Chapel Parish. Pastor James Fadel would combine his secular job at Ford with pastoring the church.

Shortly after, in June 1992, a second US parish of the RCCG called International Chapel was established in Tallahassee, Florida, by another Nigerian couple, Olu Obed and his wife, Elsie. The third US parish of the RCCG was established in Dallas, Texas, in 1994 and led by Pastor Ajibike Akinkoye, a university lecturer from Nigeria.

These initial three parishes of the RCCG in the US later proliferated. As of this writing, there are over 1,600 RCCG parishes across North America, South America, and the islands of the Caribbean. RCCG America Continent One (ACO) comprises the United States,

Central America, and the countries of the Caribbean Islands, with a total of 1,104 parishes. RCCG America Continent Two (ACT) comprises Canada, Mexico, and the nations of the South American continent, with a total of 550 parishes.

The Church in Canada

Pastor Daniel Ishola, a member of the RCCG in Nigeria, migrated to Toronto, Ontario, in November 1994, not as a pastor or missionary but in search of the proverbial greener pasture. On his arrival, Pastor Ishola sought a parish of the church in which to worship and eventually discovered that there was none in Toronto or anywhere in Canada. As part of his training as a worker of RCCG in Nigeria, he was encouraged—along with other members of RCCG, namely, sisters Bisi Odukoya and Mrs. Lee—to start a house fellowship in Toronto. In May 1995, they commenced a fellowship that met every Wednesday at a mall food court in Scarborough. Shortly afterwards, the informal house fellowship meetings metamorphosed into a steady congregational meeting. Pastor Ayo Adeloye travelled to Toronto from the United States in 1995 to formally inaugurate the RCCG in Canada at Quality Inn Scarborough. Twenty persons attended the dedication.

The RCCG in Canada received support and encouragement from RCCG pastors in the USA, namely Pastors Toye Ademola, Dave Okunade, and Ajibike Akinkoye. They took turns flying in from Texas to Toronto to minister to the new church. In May 1996, RCCG Covenant Chapel in Toronto was formally dedicated to the Lord as the first RCCG church in Canada by the general overseer, pastor E.A. Adeboye. Pastor Daniel Ishola was also confirmed as the first Parish Pastor of Covenant Chapel Toronto.

In 1997, The Lord impressed it upon Pastor Daniel Ishola that he should go and take over the capital of Canada. RCCG Overcomers Parish, Ottawa, was planted. Those who played key roles and assisted in moulding RCCG Overcomers Parish, Ottawa, included Sister Idowu, a former staff at the Nigerian High Commission in Ottawa; Adetokunboh Aluko, Abimbola Akinfenwa, and Tope Oderinde, all of whom were students at the University of Ottawa; and Bro Ayeire.

Since 1994, God has prospered His work in Canada. What started as a fellowship of three has blossomed into over 250 parishes across fifty-five zones, fourteen provinces, and four regions. The administrative headquarters of the church in Canada is in Brampton, Ontario.

Leadership in the Americas: Continent II, Region 1 (ACT 1)

PASTOR FEMI OLAWALE
Continental Overseer
RCCG Americas Continent II, Region 1 (ACT 1)
Leadership, Training and Development

Pastor Femi Olawale serves in various leadership capacities in the Redeemed Christian Church of God. He is the Senior Pastor of RCCG Overcomers' Chapel in Ottawa. He serves as the Regional Pastor and has served as Country Coordinator for RCCG Canada, providing spiritual leadership and counsel to over two hundred churches. He also served as the Deputy Continental Overseer for RCCG in the Americas before his present position as the Continental Overseer for RCCG Americas Continent II.

Pastor Olawale is a solid teacher of the word who has served in ministry for over thirty years. His drive over all these years has been sustained by his unwavering belief in the infallibility of God's word. This belief is deeply entrenched in his teachings and can be imparted to the heart of any believer who listens to him. God has been faithful to transform many lives through his ministry. He believes God to a fault and is well known for the phrase "impossibility does not exist with God."

Prior to his leadership roles in the church, he was well established in the corporate world as a skilled entrepreneur. He holds various degrees, including a Bachelor's in Mechanical Engineering, a Master's in Business Administration, and a PhD in Organizational Leadership. There was no clear-cut transition from the corporate world to ministry because he has always operated in both worlds. However, as a shepherd of the Lord's sheep, he finds fulfillment in teaching, admonishing, correcting, and leading the flock in his care with love and Godly wisdom.

Pastor Femi Olawale is married to Pastor Bukky, and they are blessed with two children. They each served as our Zonal Coordinator in Zone 17, ON 3, and they now serve as our regional pastors.

PASTOR BUKKY OLAWALE
Co–Continental Overseer
RCCG Americas Continent II, Region 1 (ACT 1)
Women, Children and Hospitality

Pastor Bukky Olawale, fondly called Mummy Pastor, has a master's degree in chemistry. She is a dedicated woman of God with an unquenchable passion for the things of God. She is exceptionally talented in bringing out the best in everyone she comes across and helping people fulfill their God-given destiny. She has a passion for ministering to women and a soft spot for young adults and children, bearing in mind that they are the future.

Pastor Bukky and her husband, best friend, mentor, and coach, Pastor Femi Olawale, co-pastor RCCG Overcomers' Chapel, located in Canada's capital city, Ottawa.

CHAPTER THREE

RCCG in Atlantic Canada

"I know your works.
See, I have set before you an open door, and no one can shut it;
for you have a little strength, have kept My word, and have not
denied My name."
—Revelation 3:8

Atlantic Canada has been inhabited for thousands of years. For at least five hundred generations, the region was home to Aboriginal Algonquian peoples. French and English colonists in North America subsequently fought for control of the region. The provinces we know today—Nova Scotia, New Brunswick, Prince Edward Island, and Newfoundland—were divided up and named by the British. Nevertheless, the Atlantic provinces retain Aboriginal, French, British, Scottish, and Gaelic influences, and tradition is highly valued here.

In the last 150 years, changes in technology have diminished traditional Atlantic industries such as fishing, lumber, and shipbuilding, contributing to economic hardship in the region. Moreover, the population of the Atlantic provinces is small compared to that of most of the other provinces. Yet it is encouraging to note that, since 2002, the yearly number of immigrants to Atlantic Canada has tripled, reaching a record 8,300 in 2015. In that time, the proportion of newcomers to Canada who settled in Atlantic Canada has almost tripled.

Such is the setting where RCCG has played a role in ministering to immigrants and others. It has not always been easy, but much has been achieved by the grace of God. Following are the stories of the first parishes in Atlantic Canada.

Into Nova Scotia: Jesus House, Halifax
by Pastor Gladys Omamofe

Jesus House Halifax, the very first parish in Atlantic Canada, had its first service on Sunday, August 12, 2007, in the old dining room of Dalhousie University, 6230 Coburg Road, Halifax. About fifteen persons heard the first message, "Resting in His Promise, and in His Presence," which ushered RCCG into Atlantic Canada. The second and last service there, "The Turning Point," was delivered one week later, on Sunday, August 19. Dalhousie University cancelled the rental of their facility, contrary to the contract signed.

Dr. and Mrs. Boboye offered the church their home on Gottingen Street in the interim, from Sunday, September 9 to Sunday, October 28, 2007. Pastors Simeon and Juliet Fagbile were residents of Halifax. They very graciously allowed the first house fellowship to begin in their home in Dartmouth. They also facilitated attendance support for the first service. More support came. Jesus House Halifax secured a small commercial space at 2358 Gottingen Street, and services began there on Sunday, November 4, 2007. This facility space was 500 square feet, and the monthly rent was $500 all-inclusive. The adult auditorium could seat a maximum of thirty persons, while the children's department room capacity was limited to ten persons.

Pioneer members of RCCG Jesus House Halifax included Brother Idowu Ogunsulire, Sister Emem Ukpong, Chinemerem Dennar, Sister Olaide Ojomo, Brother Segun Falusi, Brother Adeola Adebayo, Brother Rufus Alubankudi, Brother Layi Aladejebi, Mrs. Taiwo Akinsiku, Sister Kate Edu (now Maduakolam), Mr. and Mrs. Adedeji, Rachael Idowu, Sister Fejiro Isukuru (now Nwankwo), Brother Alex Nwankwo, Sister Lola Aladejebi (now Adeyemi), Mrs. Agnes Aladejebi, and Brother Maxwell Ejelike. All these people (less the first five) are still members of the church today.

Still in 2007, Pastor Femi Olawale introduced me, Pastor Gladys Omamofe, to Pastors Gbenga and Bisi Adenuga. Accompanied by their three children, Pastors Gbenga and Bisi came from Moncton, New

Brunswick, most Sundays to give support to the struggling new parish. Pastor Gbenga would give the sermon while Pastor Bisi taught in the children's Sunday school.

By 2009, Jesus House Halifax had outgrown its space on Gottingen Street. For about two years, it was challenging getting a suitable facility for the church. At the 2011 convention in Toronto came the word that brought the breakthrough. The general overseer, Pastor E.A. Adeboye, said, "There is a miracle waiting for you at home." I claimed it. Everything moved unbelievably fast afterwards. God broke all protocols, and we secured the facility at 2760 Robie Street. Fifty congregants moved into the new facility by faith on October 1, 2011. The facility was 2,550 square feet, and the rent was $6,745.28 monthly.

In 2012, the superintendent for the Halifax Regional Police invited us to set up a community food bank in the Gottingen neighbourhood. With his team of officers, they collaborated with us and arranged for the Halifax Regional Municipality (HRM) Housing to give us an apartment, rent-free. They painted, provided furniture, and connected us with Feed Nova Scotia. Jesus House Food Bank, an associate member of Feed Nova Scotia, remains one of our thriving Corporate Social Responsibility (CSR) initiatives. In addition, we support daily feeding in our community by collaborating with Hope Cottage. Meals are cooked and served twice daily. We also support Souls Harbour in their own feeding program in another community initiative. Our YAYA members volunteer from time to time at Souls Harbour Mart Thrift Store, supporting their charity work. Annually, we hold Easter Saturday Crusade (since 2018) and July 1st Canada Day Crusade (since 2021) as open-air evangelistic events with live bands and sharing of tracts, bibles, and personal ministrations at Victoria Park, a central park in the city.

Since 2019/2020, we have been holding three Sunday services: two for adults and children, and a third service later in the afternoon for teenagers and youths in the colleges and universities. This is because of space constraints and the inability to secure a bigger venue. The parish has been seeking to buy its own property. Our youth church, Berean Youths, is going strong. Service is still held every Sunday afternoon. In transit to our permanent place of worship, we currently worship at the Atlantica Hotel at 1980 Robie Street in Halifax.

The vision of RCCG Jesus House Halifax is to raise a transformed community of discipled believers who live like Jesus and share His love, and to impact our community through the transforming power of the Holy Spirit in sound Biblical teaching, true worship, consistent prayer, and evangelism.

Pastor Gladys Omamofe
RCCG Jesus House
PO Box 40008 Robie St. RPO, Halifax, NS B3K 0E4
Phone: (902) 210-6060 (cell)
www.rccgjhhalifax.org

Into New Brunswick: Cornerstone Chapel, Moncton
by Pastors Gbenga and Bisi Adenuga

The inception of the Redeemed Christian Church of God Cornerstone Chapel Moncton (CCM) traces back to the visionary leadership of Pastor Gbenga Adenuga, an ordained Assistant Pastor at the time, and his wife, Pastor Bisi Adenuga, an ordained Deaconess.

The inaugural service was held in Brother Godefroid's and Sister Lillian Ilunga's basement on November 16, 2008, where seven adults and ten children gathered for worship as we awaited the purchase of our proposed church building at 11 York Street, which was finalized in January 2009. The building's loan was secured by Gbenga and Bisi Adenuga and Dr. and Mrs. Soyege (our Assistant Pastors in Hlatikulu, Swaziland), who reside in Alberta, Canada. The loan was later converted to a term loan secured by Pastors Gbenga and Bisi Adenuga and Dr. Busola Akinmokun to relieve the Soyeges of the loan burden. Our first major building-related challenge surfaced in April 2009, after the snow thawed and several leaks in the basement of the building led to flooding and significant expenses which were not covered by insurance.

Cornerstone Chapel Moncton became the Atlantic area headquarters in March 2009 under the leadership of Pastor Olawale. The church was officially inaugurated with Pastor Femi Olawale's dedication of the new building and a celebration from May 22 to 24, 2009. The event was graced by city dignitaries and esteemed guests, including Pastor Yinka Dada from Hamilton, Ontario; Pastor Gladys Omamofe from Halifax, Nova Scotia; and all our brethren from Nova Scotia, Prince Edward Island, and all across New Brunswick, too numerous to mention one by one.

Despite the building's capacity of two hundred, our congregation averaged only eighteen attendees, including children, for over five years. The early years were not without their share of challenges. High turnover, slow growth, new church planting with few members, and a significant house fellowship breakaway tested our faith. However, our unyielding belief and reliance on the Holy Spirit's guidance fortified our resolve, demonstrating the resilience of our church community.

As a sponsorship agreement holder with Citizenship and Immigration Canada, Cornerstone sponsored a family of five refugees to Moncton in 2013. The cookbooks produced for the support of this endeavour are a constant reminder of how God can use small things to achieve big results.

In 2014, Cornerstone achieved a significant milestone by introducing interpretation of our sermon into French, officially making the church a bilingual church accessible to the French-speaking community. This development propelled our numbers beyond the twenty-mark barrier and made our church a more inclusive and diverse place of worship.

Today, our church is a vibrant hub of worship and community. We conduct four services every Sunday, each catering to a specific group. In the morning, we have two adult sessions running concurrently with the children's church, providing spiritual nourishment for the whole family. In the afternoon, the Royal Connections young adults group holds their service, fostering a sense of belonging and growth among our young adults. The Royal Masterpiece teenagers meet in the evening, guiding our young members on their spiritual journey. A new addition to the Cornerstone family is our campus fellowship, Royal

Campus Connection, which is held every Saturday evening at Mount Allison University campus, shining the light of the gospel on campus.

As part of our social responsibility to the community, Cornerstone Neighbourhood Outreach shares messages of hope and Christ's love to the community through Easter and Christmas drives. This effort has evolved from a humble beginning to a separately registered entity, Atlantic Hope Ambassadors.

As a testament of God's faithfulness, CCM has outgrown its present facility at 11 York Street and secured 4.38 acres of virgin land for the construction of a multi-million-dollar 1,374-seat auditorium in a 50,000-square-foot, multipurpose, multi-generational facility at 199 Price Street in Moncton, New Brunswick. This complex, the first of its kind in Atlantic Canada, will include a worship center, a daycare, an indoor sports field, conference and meeting rooms, a gym, a children's indoor play area, a café, a photo studio, an industrial kitchen, and an event center. Construction is expected to begin this year. The new building, rightly named The Light House, will cater to the needs of the growing community.

The mission of The Redeemed Christian Church of God Cornerstone Chapel Moncton (CCM) is to equip people with power to pursue their purpose with passion and perseverance.

Our flagship programs include virtual weekday prayer meetings from 6:00 to 6:30 am, the Cornerstone Bethel experience at 6:00 am the first Saturday of every month, and our monthly testimony and communion service at 6:00 pm every first Sunday. Cornerstone's midweek teaching services go deeper into the word. Other programs include Friendship Sunday (the first Sunday in March) and Diversity Sunday to mark Canada Day (the first Sunday in July).

As we reflect on the journey from humble beginnings to the flourishing community we are today, we are filled with gratitude. In drought and abundance, the Lord has demonstrated His faithfulness, empowering us to fulfill His divine purpose. We are grateful for every member of our church community who has contributed to our growth and success. Cornerstone Chapel Moncton recently partnered with four other denominational churches in the city of Moncton for the first joint Good Friday service attended by diverse Christian worshippers.

Let somebody shout, "Hallelujah!"

Pastors Gbenga and Bisi Adenuga
RCCG Cornerstone Chapel
11 York St., Moncton, NB E1C 2Y2
Phone: (506) 855-7224
www.ccm.church

Into Prince Edward Island: Living Word Assembly, Charlottetown

The Redeemed Christian Church of God Living Word Assembly (LWA) was founded in 2013. The first service and inauguration of the parish was on Sunday, September 8, 2013. Before the inauguration of the parish, Pastor Abiodun and Pastor Mrs. Yemi Olusoji hosted a house fellowship meeting in their house on Sunset Drive in Charlottetown. The house fellowship had an encouraging number of people attending regularly. However, as soon as the parish was started, many people realized the necessity of commitment to the work that had just started, and they stopped attending the service. But that didn't discourage Pastor Abiodun and Pastor Yemi Olusoji. They persevered faithfully with the work, and the Lord progressively brought more people to His light. RCCG LWA was initially meeting at the Murphy Community Centre. We had a room that could barely seat twenty people, and each Sunday, we had to negotiate for a bigger space. We also had to move equipment every Sunday.

In April 2014, Brother John Cuma accepted a professional job offer in Charlottetown. Consequently, he and his wife, Sister Rebecca Cuma, relocated to Charlottetown from Moncton, New Brunswick. While in Moncton, John and Rebecca Cuma were workers in RCCG Cornerstone Chapel Moncton, so naturally they joined the workforce at Living Word

Assembly in Charlottetown. As God would have it in His divine plan, infinite Grace and Mercy, when it was time for Pastor Abiodun and Pastor Yemi to relocate to Ontario, Canada, on July 10, 2016, the mantle for pastoring RCCG Living Word Assembly Charlottetown was handed over to Brother John and Sister Rebecca.

In 2017, we moved to our current location with a capacity of one hundred people. However, we have outgrown the space, and we are believing God for our own permanent location. As a child of God, you can partner with Him on His project by donating via eTransfer to building@lwa.church or online at www.lwa.church. God has been faithful; we have grown not only numerically but spiritually as well, desiring to know God, to be used by God, and to enjoy God. The population of the church is predominantly (about 80 percent) undergraduate students. Each year, as they graduate and relocate to other cities to work, God in his miraculous ways keeps adding unto us and maturing his people as the work is increasing. It is a very humbling experience.

Coming out of the COVID-19 pandemic was like rebuilding the church, but the testimony is that God is with us; He's always been. He has not allowed the enemy to have victory over us. LWA has a few special programs, including A Night of Worship and Breakthrough Prayers, among others. A Night of Worship started in 2016. It is a believers' meeting where we gather to worship God and experience fellowship with The Holy Spirit, with no prayer requesting. Breakthrough Prayers came as an instruction from God as we were coming out of the lockdown and people were facing various kinds of challenging issues. Breakthrough Prayers is a time of intensive fellowship with God and prayers to achieve a breakthrough. We soak ourselves in His presence for eight hours. As children of God, we are to be a light in this dark world. God has high interest in our lives. God is still in the business of healing the sick and raising the dead; however, He is more interested in building an intimate relationship with us.

The Glory of the Lord is risen upon RCCG Living Word Assembly Charlottetown. The people of Prince Edward Island are coming to her light and kings to the brightness of her rising. We are reintroducing our Lord

Jesus Christ and the potency of the Power of the Holy Spirit that raised Him from the dead. We want to become like Jesus, fulfilling destiny, winning souls, making heaven, and taking as many people as possible with us.

Pastors John and Rebecca Cuma
RCCG Living Word Assembly
4-99 Pownal Street, Charlottetown, PE C1A 3W4
Phone: (902) 982-0926
www.lwa.church

Into Newfoundland and Labrador: Mount Zion, St. John's
by Pastors Akinyemi and Olufunmilayo Familusi

RCCG Mount Zion Parish started as a house fellowship unit on May 24, 2014, with six brethren in attendance and two children who were also growing in the Lord. The house fellowship was born out of passion for the souls of brethren of like mind and passion and great desire for fellowship with them. Obadiah 1:17—"But on Mount Zion there shall deliverance, And there shall be holiness; The house of Jacob shall possess their possessions." The house fellowship continued to grow, and by January 2015, the plan to start a full parish of Mount Zion in St. John's, Newfoundland, was in motion with great encouragement from our mother parish, RCCG Mount Zion, in the State of Kuwait. The initial desire was fully supported and guidance provided by our then Provincial Pastor, Pastor Yinka Dada (PYD); our Zonal Pastor, Pastor Gbenga Adenuga; and our Area Pastor, Pastor Gladys Omamofe. All these wonderful men and woman of God supported us prayerfully and were available to provide us with needed advice at every point. We appreciate them as always.

The RCCG Mount Zion parish started on June 7, 2015, in the sitting room at 9 Thetis Place, St. John's, Newfoundland, the home of our pastors, the Familusis. The total attendance at our first service was twelve (five women, two men, and five children). The topic of the message was Wonders of Praise, the preacher was Olufunmilayo Familusi, and the total offering collected was CAD$44.00. The founding members were Pastor Olufunmilayo Familusi, Brother Precious Familusi, Dr. Emmanuel Asapo, Sister Medeseh Asapo, Sister Omotola Ojerinde, Sister Toluwani Okoye (née Familusi), and Sister Enohor. The children present at the first service were Promise Asapo, Fikayo Ojerinde, Emmanuel Ojerinde, Onomeh and Chinwe.

We continued to encourage ourselves with the scripture "Though your beginning was small, Yet your latter end would increase abundantly" (Job 8:7). The church began to grow in His Grace. After five months, the whole house could not contain us, and we were left with only the option to move to a bigger venue. With God's favour, we were granted access to the Crosbie building at our community centre, the NL Sports Centre. We moved to this venue on December 6, 2015. The church continued to grow in His Grace, and by the end of the first quarter of 2017, the community center was becoming too small for us and the children as God was adding to His church.

Trusting God, we moved to a commercial building. The rent sounded high, but we continued trusting God, and the slogan among the leaders then was, "If God sends us on this mission, He will surely fund us." At this point, we were resting one hundred percent on God's provision. To the Glory of His name, we never had reason to borrow or raise special funds to pay rent. The Lord was blessing His people and His Church, the church was growing in numbers, and God was supplying our needs according to His own riches.

Prior to the COVID-19 pandemic, we were already having challenges due to space. Then COVID-19 struck, and churches were closed. Initially we were bothered, but our leaders' slogan changed. Our new slogan was, "They shall not be ashamed in the evil time, And in the days of famine they shall be satisfied" (Psalm 37:19). We approached our landlord for a reduction in rent, but he refused. This was so annoying that we decided to look for another space, this time a permanent building for RCCG Mount Zion Parish. We started praying for insight and direction. The first space we found was beautiful but did not have enough space for an assembly. We continued our services in the rented space for a few months after COVID-19 until June 26, 2021, when we had our last service there and moved to our permanent worship centre.

Our story would not be complete if we did not narrate how God provided us with our current building. The initial challenge was getting credit approval. The financial institution turned down the application at the final stage. This was so disappointing, but God raised help for us, as the owner agreed for us to move into the building as renters with the option to purchase. We moved to this building in July 4, 2021. Within nine months of operating under the rental-to-purchase agreement, we finalized the purchase of the building. We are grateful to God, who provided us with the resources and raised men who, like Nehemiah, had the mind to build. Throughout the building acquisition and upgrading, our slogan was, "'So we built the wall, and the entire wall was joined together up to half its height, for the people had a mind to work' (Nehemiah 4:6). Join the builder." God raised builders around the globe to support the work.

God has done spectacular miracles in His church. The church that started with twelve people in attendance at the first service has grown to an average of 250 adults and 150 children. One of our sisters, who had waited for the fruit of the womb for about ten years, gave birth to twins. Long-outstanding immigration applications were approved, souls were converted, and God favoured our people tremendously in their careers and businesses.

Currently, RCCG Mount Zion St. John's NL is in the next phase of our development. God of amazing wonders is taking His church to the stage of exponential growth. Our current slogan is "No eye has seen, no ear has heard, and no mind has imagined what God has prepared for those who love him" (1 Corinthians 2:9). We will continue to love and worship Him while we wait patiently for His amazing wonders in the midst of His people.

Pastors Akinyemi and Olufunmilayo Familusi
RCCG Mount Zion
109 Blackmarsh Road, St. John's NL A1E 1S6
Phone: (709) 770-2501
www.rccgmountzionnl.org

CHAPTER FOUR

Our Leaders Along the Journey

And Moses said to the children of Israel, "See, the Lord has called by name Bezalel the son of Uri, the son of Hur, of the tribe of Judah; and He has filled him with the Spirit of God, in wisdom and understanding, in knowledge and all manner of workmanship, to design artistic works, to work in gold and silver and bronze, in cutting jewels for setting, in carving wood, and to work in all manner of artistic workmanship.
"And He has put in his heart the ability to teach, in him and Aholiab the son of Ahisamach, of the tribe of Dan. He has filled them with skill to do all manner of work of the engraver and the designer and the tapestry maker, in blue, purple, and scarlet thread, and fine linen, and of the weaver—those who do every work and those who design artistic works.
—Exodus 35:30–35

PASTOR OLAYINKA DADA
Deputy Continental Overseer
Americas Continent II, Region 2 (ACT 2)
School of Discipleship (SOD) and Men of Influence (MOI)

Pastor Olayinka Dada is currently the Deputy Continental Overseer of The Redeemed Christian Church of God (RCCG), The Americas Continent II. He is also the Senior Pastor of RCCG, Restoration House in Hamilton, Ontario, and God has used him tremendously to transform lives through sound and uncompromising teachings of the Word of God. He is a practicing physician and tent maker who loves soccer and the outdoors. Together, he and his wife, Oluwatoyin, served as our

Provincial Pastors from 2013 to 2016. They reside in Hamilton, Ontario, with their four blessed children.

PASTOR TOYIN DADA
Co–Deputy Continental Overseer
Americas Continent II, Region 2 (ACT 2)

Pastor Oluwatoyin Dada, better known as Pastor T, is fondly called the first lady at Restoration House. She has a heart for children and is passionate about directing young women in Christ to their identity as King's Daughters. She is firmly rooted in the Word and a mother at our church to many beyond her four children.

FROM THE DESK OF
Pastors Olayinka Dada and Oluwatoyin Dada
Senior Pastors, RCCG Restoration House, Hamilton, Ontario
Deputy Continental Overseer, RCCG The Americas Continent II

—Message to RCCG Atlantic Province—

In this moment of reflection, remembrance, and respect, my wife and I gratefully acknowledge the enduring goodness and faithfulness of God as evidenced in the lives of our mentees and friends, Pastors Gbenga and Bisi Adenuga, and their journey. Our paths intertwined with theirs when they relocated to Swaziland in 1998, just four years after our own move and two years following the establishment of an RCCG parish there under our guidance. Their unwavering commitment, servants' hearts, and steadfast faith shone brightly as they undertook the monumental task of initiating an RCCG parish in Swaziland. Their subsequent move to New Brunswick in 2003 mirrored our own transition to Ontario, where we embarked on a similar journey of establishing a parish.

Witnessing Adenuga's determination to plant the first RCCG parish in New Brunswick and the second in the Atlantic region in 2008 filled us with admiration. Their inauguration weekend in 2009 marked a significant milestone, one we were honored to celebrate alongside them. From humble beginnings, the work flourished, spreading to multiple zones and eventually evolving into a provincial entity. Serving as their provincial pastors from 2013 to 2016, we shared in the joy of nurturing growth and witnessing the birth of new parishes, even in what initially seemed like barren ground. During this time, the Atlantic churches experienced remarkable expansion, culminating in the launch of RADAH magazine at our provincial visit and zonal conference in 2016. It's truly remarkable to behold the transformative power of God's grace within the Atlantic region within such a brief span.

We humbly give all glory to God for His unwavering love, faithfulness, and abundant blessings throughout this journey. Our admiration for the Adenugas knows no bounds; their courage, resilience, leadership, and compassion are qualities we deeply cherish and celebrate. As our friendship continues to mature like fine wine, growing stronger and more intertwined with each passing year, we look forward to conquering new territories together, not only within the Atlantic region and Canada but also across the world at large. We are equally grateful that our father and mother in the Lord are able to pay a visit to the Atlantic region on this leg of their visit to Canada. We hope they have an amazing time in this tranquil coastal region of our beautiful nation, Canada.

PASTOR TAYO ROBERT-OJAJUNI
Assistant Continental Overseer
Americas Continent II, Region 3 (ACT 3)
Special Programs, Projects and Logistics

Pastor Tayo Robert-Ojajuni (PTRO) gradually discovered the essence of God in his life. He became the pastor of RCCG Covenant Chapel in Toronto in August 1999. While he was still working as a software engineer, a call to go into full-time ministry agitated his mind. It was a decision that took a couple of years to make. PTRO opted for God by quitting his job and going into full-time ministry in January 2005. He is now vigorously pursuing his passion by teaching the power and principle of being a victorious Christian who will impact the greater society. His vision is to Redeem Destinies and Restore Dominion. He firmly believes that as children of God in body, soul and spirit, we are marvellously made. He is an author and a publisher of many journals and articles. Pastor Tayo Robert-Ojajuni is happily married to Pastor Bunmi, and they are blessed with five children. They served as our provincial pastors from 2016 to 2019.

PASTOR BUNMI OJAJUNI
Co–Assistant Continental Overseer
Americas Continent II, Region 3 (ACT 3)

Pastor Bunmi Ojajuni (Pastor Boomstar) is the First Lady and Senior Pastor at The King's Covenant (TKC). As she walks and serves alongside her husband, PTRO, she has dedicated her life to living by example and encouraging young adults, men, and women on how to live up to their full potential and fulfill their destinies in Christ. She is a down-to-earth, jovial woman of God, which enables her to teach and counsel others with humour, warmth, transparency, and strength. Pastor Boomstar heads the Kingdom Impact Group, which consists of three ministries: Children Ministry, Women Ministry (Chayil Women), and Hospitality. Pastor Boomstar is a wife, mother, teacher, speaker, role model, and mentor. She takes pleasure in the family structure, and is happily married to her longtime sweetheart, PTRO. They are proud parents of five children: Tobi, Mowa, Timi, Moye, and Mofe.

FROM THE DESK OF
Pastors Olutayo and Olubunmi Robert-Ojajuni
RCCG Americas Continent II, Region 3

—Our Involvement with Atlantic Canada—

It is with great joy that we put this together as Atlantic Canada hosts our parents in the Lord, Pastor and Pastor Mrs. E.A. Adeboye. This is a day we have looked forward to for a long time, and we give glory to the Almighty God that we are witnessing such a glorious occasion.

We have been part of the growth and the tremendous strides in glory that Atlantic Canada has made under the leadership of Pastor and Pastor Mrs. Gbenga Adenuga. This is a couple who love the Lord and also project positively everything about The Redeemed Christian Church of God. A very important attribute of Atlantic Canada is the togetherness of the pastors in sharing the gospel of our Lord Jesus Christ in this area. The programs held are properly put together to ensure that Jesus is revealed even to the unchurched, destinies are redeemed by the quality of the programs, dominion is restored by the intentionality of the leaders, and Jesus is ultimately glorified.

It is significant to note that Atlantic Canada values feedback. They have come to realize that feedback ignored could be strange fire ignited; therefore, after every program, they dissect what has been done to ensure that lessons are learnt and errors are not perpetuated. Even though we are not directly involved with the administration of Atlantic Canada anymore, our relationship with the leaders transcends formal structures. Therefore, we are still able to chip in one or two things with respect to the growth of the Atlantic region and the visit of our parents in the Lord to ensure that they are comfortable and will look forward to coming to Atlantic Canada again if their schedule permits and Jesus tarries in his return.

To all the leaders and members of RCCG in Atlantic Canada, we congratulate you. Always remember that, in the words of Roy T. Bennett, "Your hardest times often lead to the greatest moments of your life.

Keep going. Tough situations build strong people in the end." No matter what God has revealed to you or whatever your aim is, let the Almighty God be your guide. "I know, Lord, that a person's way of life is not his own; no one who walks determines his own steps" (Jeremiah 10:23, CSB). If you believe it, behave it, and you will eventually become it. Be Blessed!

PASTOR OLUDARE AYENI
Special Assistant to the Continental Overseer (SATCO)
Pastor in Charge of Province (PICP)
Americas Continent II, Region 1, Province 1 (ACT 1, P1)
Sunday School and House Fellowship

Pastor Oludare Ayeni has served in various capacities in the Redeemed Christian Church of God, where he has been a Pastor for over twenty-five years. He was the pioneer Pastor of the mission in the province of Quebec, Canada, and currently, he is the Senior Pastor of RCCG Chapel of Grace in Ottawa. He is the Pastor in Charge (PICP) of Province 1 Region 1 in the Americas Continent II (ACT), where he also serves as the Special Assistant to the Continental Overseer (SATCO) in charge of Sunday school and house fellowship.

Pastor Ayeni is a graduate of the Redeemed Bible College in Ebute Meta, Lagos, Nigeria, and he was the parish pastor of Mercy Parish, Ibesse Ikorodu, Lagos, before relocating to Canada in 2000. His keen interest is teaching the total counsel of the word of God, especially holiness and obedience to the word of God and to constituted authorities. His favourite event in the church is Bible study (Digging Deep). Pastor Oludare Ayeni worked in the banking industry in Nigeria. In Canada, he has worked as an accountant with various organizations in banking, private corporations, and not-for-profit organizations, which he found very rewarding because of his passion for community service.

Pastor Oludare Ayeni is married to Pastor Oyinlola Ayeni. The pastors served as our zonal coordinators from 2011 to 2013 and as our provincial pastors from 2019 to 2022.

PASTOR OYINLOLA AYENI
Co–Pastor in Charge of Province (PICP)
Americas Continent II, Region 1, Province 1 (ACT 1, P1)

Pastor Oyinlola Ayeni is a passionate teacher of the word and a consummate prayer warrior. Her ministry interest is in children, youth education and mentoring. Pastor Lola is an intercessor, a wise counsellor, an efficient planner, and an administrator endowed with immense initiative and a great capacity for hard work. She is a leader, full of zeal and excellence, and a blessing to womanhood. She challenges and encourages women to fulfill their calling and purpose in life and ministry. She is a role model to the new generation of youths and a dedicated mentor to many people. She co-pastors RCCG Chapel of Grace Ottawa alongside her husband, Pastor Oludare Ayeni, the Pastor in Charge in Province 1, ACT-1 region. They are blessed with three godly children: a girl and two boys.

FROM THE DESK OF
Pastors Oludare and Oyinlola Ayeni
Pastors in Charge of Province (PICP),
Americas Continent II (ACT), Region 1 Province 1

—Letter to RCCG Atlantic Province—

I heartily congratulate you on this auspicious visit of our father in the Lord, the General Overseer of the RCCG worldwide, Pastor E.A. Adeboye, and our Mother in the Lord, Pastor Mrs. Folu Adeboye, to Atlantic Canada.

RCCG in Atlantic Canada has indeed come a long way, from an area to a zone and now a province. I met Atlantic Canada as an area when

I became the Ontario 3 Zonal Co-ordinator in 2011. The zone then stretched from Eastern Ontario (Kingston) to Ottawa, the whole of Quebec, and the Atlantic. I used to love coming to the Atlantic in those days. My annual zonal visit was always like a homecoming of sorts. As God will arrange it, Pastor Gbenga Adenuga was then the Area Pastor, and I chose him, I believe by divine providence, to serve as my Assistant Zonal Coordinator. One thing unique about the pastors and members of the Atlantic churches is the zeal they put into the programmes of the zonal conferences. The planning and richness of the programmes, from real bible teaching to such side attractions as soccer and athletic games, made me look forward to coming to the Atlantic.

As time moved on, the Atlantic was made a zone, and I was not able to visit for some time. But the opportunity for us to connect again came in 2020, when I became a provincial pastor with oversight in the Atlantic. We were able to take up our relationship from where we stopped, and I enjoyed the brief time we had together before the Atlantic, justifiably, was made a province. I must mention that, of all areas and zones under me then, the Atlantic occupies a very special place in my memory. From the cooperation I enjoyed to the quality and variety of the programmes during my visits, I will not forget it in a hurry.

Our last visit to the Atlantic before they became a province is very special to me, because my wife has a very special bond with Pastor Bisi Adenuga. I am especially very fond of many pastors in the Atlantic for their commitment to the work, their industry, and their genuine love for us. I bear them witness that they loved us. I wish the Atlantic a great blessing from the General Overseer's visit, and I pray for the continued health of all the churches, the pastors, and all members under the leadership of Pastors Gbenga and Bisi Adenuga and those who hold their hands up in the service of our Lord and saviour Jesus Christ. God bless you all, and, once again, congratulations.

PASTOR GBENGA ADENUGA
Area Pastor, 2009–2013
Zonal Coordinator, 2013–2022
Pastor in Charge of Province, October 2022–present

Pastor Gbenga Adenuga pioneered Cornerstone Chapel Moncton in November 2008. Prior to that, he served as the founding and residing pastor of RCCG Overcomer's parish in Hlatikulu, Swaziland, from August 2001 to June 2003. He immigrated to Canada in July 2003 and immediately made himself available to serve at Glad Tidings Pentecostal Church, serving as a Sunday school teacher and a member of the board of deacons.

The attributes that best describe Pastor Gbenga are his strong motivational teaching and focus on excellence, leadership, and youth development and counselling. His primary focus is to equip people with the power of the word to pursue their purpose with the kind of passion and perseverance he exemplifies. He has a burning desire to see members connect and care about the needs of those around them. Pastor Gbenga is bivocational and continues to practice medicine in Moncton. He is the husband of Bisi Adenuga, and they are blessed with three victorious children: Ore, Posi, and Tofunmi.

PASTOR BISI ADENUGA
Area Pastor, 2009–2013
Zonal Coordinator, 2013–2022
Pastor in Charge of Province, October 2022–present

Pastor Bisi Adenuga co-pioneered Cornerstone Chapel Moncton with her husband, Pastor Gbenga Adenuga, in November 2008. Prior to that, she served as founding and children's pastor of RCCG Overcomer's parish in Hlatikulu, Swaziland, from August 2001 to June 2003. She holds a master's degree in theology. Pastor Bisi is a woman of prayer with a big heart for women and children. She takes soul-winning and community very seriously, spending the first hours of her day focused on prayer and bible study and preparation to be active where God is at work. She is actively involved in her community, promoting diversity and inclusion through generosity, dedication, volunteerism, and hard work. Pastor Bisi works as a registered nurse, a certified diabetic educator, and a lifestyle coach. She manages her husband's medical practice, and she will do anything to make sure all her children (biological and spiritual) become the best in life.

In 2017, Pastors Gbenga and Bisi Adenuga were jointly awarded a Senate of Canada Sesquicentennial Medal in recognition of their positive contributions to the lives of immigrants to New Brunswick. Through their work, they have helped newcomers from over twenty different nationalities become integrated members of the community. In collaboration with the Multicultural Association of the Greater Moncton Area (MAGMA), Dr. Adenuga also supervised Refugee Health Moncton, a program to help improve the health of government-assisted refugees.

OUR LEADERS ALONG THE JOURNEY

Pastor Tayo Ojajuni, ACT 3 Assistant Continental Overseer
(Special Programs, Projects and Logistics)

Pastor Oludare Ayeni, SATCO (Sunday School and
House Fellowship), ACT 1, Province 1

Pastors in Charge of the Atlantic Provinces, Gbenga and Bisi Adenuga

Pastors Simeon and Juliet Fagbile, AT1 Zone Coordinator 1

Pastor Gladys Omamofe, AT1 Zone Coordinator 2

CHAPTER FIVE

Growth of RCCG in Atlantic Canada

"Enlarge the place of your tent,
And let them stretch out the curtains of your dwellings;
Do not spare;
Lengthen your cords,
And strengthen your stakes.
For you shall expand to the right and to the left,
And your descendants will inherit the nations,
And make the desolate cities inhabited.
"Do not fear, for you will not be ashamed;
Neither be disgraced, for you will not be put to shame;
For you will forget the shame of your youth,
And will not remember the reproach of your widowhood anymore.
For your Maker is *your husband,*
The Lord of hosts is *His name;*
And your Redeemer is *the Holy One of Israel;*
He is called the God of the whole earth.
—Isaiah 54:2–5

RCCG RESTORATION CHAPEL HALIFAX, NOVA SCOTIA

Restoration Chapel started under the leadership of Pastors Simeon and Fayoke Olugbile on March 1, 2009. The church was inaugurated on the same day by Pastor Femi Olawale, the current Continental Overseer for RCCG Americas Continent II, and supported by the presence of our Provincial Pastor, Gbenga Adenuga. We had about eighty persons in attendance at our inaugural service, where family and friends rejoiced that a new work of grace had started. The place of worship was located at 180 Greystone Housing Estate for low-income persons and refugees from Africa, a duplex building called Halifax Metro Housing which was given to the Salvation Army for Women program and then subleased to Restoration Chapel.

In this new area, we had only people who were dependent on the little income of the church. We had families of limited means—nevertheless, very spiritual and dedicated—from the following nationalities: Belize (1 international student), Bermuda (1 international student), Cameroon (1 family), Canada (2 individuals), Democratic Republic of Congo (1 family), Jamaica (1 family), Liberia (3 families), Rwanda (1 family), and Togo (4 families).

By the church's first anniversary, we had become a symbol of the African nations and exceeded the licensed capacity of our space at Halifax Metro Housing. Consequently, we moved to the Captain Spry Community Centre, but the constant bank-holiday closures of the building facility during festival times created a substantial hindrance to our church's numerical growth. During our first anniversary celebration, Pastor Tayo Ojajuni was our guest minister from Toronto. He compelled the young church to move its location, as it was not conducive for worship services due to the overwhelming noise and distractions from the other users of the community centre accessing its swimming pool. As a result, we began alternating between the basement of the pastor's residence and the Captain Spry Community Centre. The decision to use the pastor's basement was a necessity due to the church's limited financial capacity to rent any space for fellowship. Later, the church relocated to Halifax Wedding Chapel at 2 Auburn Drive in Spryfield. After worshipping out of that location for close to one year, the landlord decided to shut down the location (she was travelling to her own country), which led us back to the basement of the pastor's residence once again.

In 2012, we took the biggest step of faith by renting a 3,500-square-foot facility at 17 Alma Crescent that housed us for three years. We really did not know where the $3,500 monthly rent would come from because the total tithes and offerings were not enough to pay the rent at that time. Many times, the church defaulted on its rental payment and church members were locked out. On several occasions, the pastor resorted to using personal funds to cover the shortfalls because he had guaranteed the lease, and the contract was duly signed by him as a private guarantor rather than by a church entity.

One Thanksgiving Sunday, we came to worship, but we discovered we had been locked out of the church facility and the landlord had removed all our signposts while publicly humiliating us for defaulted payments. An unknown man—to this day, we still call him "The Mystery Man"—came to our rescue as the landlord was verbally and physically aggressive towards us even when we had already told him about our intention to vacate. This mystery man promised and guaranteed the landlord the rent would be paid when due. This man paid the rent for a year and two months, when we finally grew in membership. The man also sent us checks for children's outings to parks and zoos, all expenses paid. I called him an angel in human clothing and a helper of destiny because when the time came to reimburse him, the address turned out to be fake and every effort to locate him proved unsuccessful. This was one of the biggest surprises of ministry that God could send an angel in human clothing, an unknown entity, to secure His church from embarrassment and collapse. The next day, the pastor's sermon was with vigour and liberty because of God's intervention: "What God ordained, God sustained."

Other minor challenges with the church were members' moving and the instability of workers, which disrupted our growth and development. Through it all, we thank God. We took another step of faith and moved to another location—334 Herring Cove Road—in 2014. This move gave us growth and impetus to create several ministry programs for children, youth, and adults. The initial rental payments were so hard, but God provided men and women with resources that helped our growth.

"And the word of God increased; and the number of the disciples multiplied in Jerusalem greatly; and a great company of the priests were obedient to the faith." (Acts 6:7)

Our growth was so phenomenal. We had doubled our size within the first year. We spent ten years of fruitful service, touching lives and destinies as we followed our mission statement, "Restoring lives and

Destinies through the proclamations of the Word." Of late, the Glory Cloud is moving again. We have moved to a 20,000-square-foot location that costs $13,800 a month. We are actively looking for a place of worship that will ensure continued growth and prosperity. Our basic challenge is accommodation, and we believe God will usher in more growth and prosperity for the church and glorify His Holy name. Amen!

Pastors Simeon and Juliet Fagbile
RCCG Restoration Chapel Halifax
334 Herring Cove Road, Halifax NS B3R 1V7
Phone: (902) 809-2366, (902) 210-2366
www.restorationchapel.ca

RCCG PAVILION OF REDEMPTION, SAINT JOHN, NEW BRUNSWICK

The Redeemed Christian Church of God (RCCG) Pavilion of Redemption in Saint John, New Brunswick, has a rich history of growth and service to the community. It all began with Pastor Grace Okonrende's visit to Saint John in August and September 2008, when she encouraged the Aladetoyinbo family to start a house fellowship. This small gathering, which began in their residence at Rothesay around October 2009, laid the foundation for what would later become the RCCG Pavilion of Redemption.

In September 2010, Pastor John Adegbenjo and Pastor Mrs. Felicia Adegbenjo, experienced church planters, were transferred from Romania to Canada. Their arrival marked a significant turning point as the house fellowship at the Aladetoyinbo residence evolved into a church. The first service was held in October 2010 with just two families in attendance. Despite its humble beginnings, the church began to grow rapidly under the leadership of Pastors John and Felicia Adegbenjo.

The church services soon outgrew the Aladetoyinbo residence and moved to the Colonial Inn, a hotel in Saint John. The Adegbenjos' fervent evangelism efforts led to a diverse and growing membership, reflecting the community's embrace of the church's message. One of the significant milestones was the church's outreach to university students, which began in 2011. This initiative not only strengthened the relationship with the students but also became one of the areas in which the parish excelled, all by the grace of God. With the membership of the church growing significantly, in August 2012, the church was able to purchase a building and move its activities from the hotel to a more suitable location. This was a testament to the church's growth and impact on the community. In the summer of 2012, Pastor William Onososen and his family moved from Ontario to join the parish. Pastor William began assisting Pastor Adegbenjo and later took over as parish pastor when the Adegbenjos received a call to start a new parish in Medicine Hat, Alberta, in the summer of 2014.

Under Pastor William's leadership, the church continued to make strides in spreading the good news of salvation. The Annual Life Conference, which began in 2014, has been a successful event, along with other initiatives such as the Young Adults Ministry, the Men's Ministry, the Women's Ministry, and teenage and children's ministries.

In February 2018, by the grace and help of God, the church moved to its current place of worship, a former Catholic church with a seating capacity of over 600 worshippers. Since then, the church has continued to grow, supporting its members and the community of Saint John. Outreach programs include youth discipleship programs, a summer Bible camp, a food bank partnership, an Overflow community dinner program, and free income tax filing assistance for low-income individuals. The church also offers short-term accommodations for newcomers and refugees to Saint John.

As we look back with gratitude for what God has done, the church also looks forward with hope and trust for what He will continue to do in the coming years. To God be the glory.

Pastors William and Dayo Onososen
RCCG Pavilion of Redemption
603 Loch Lomond Rd, Saint John NB E2J 1Y8
Phone: (506) 343-6116
www.rccgsj.org

RCCG PRAISE CHAPEL, FREDERICTON, NEW BRUNSWICK

RCCG Praise Chapel Fredericton was birthed in 2012 by the inspiration of God. The Pioneer Pastor, Pastor Anthony Idode Iluebbey, arrived in Fredericton, New Brunswick, as a missionary from Nigeria in March 2012 and established a house fellowship centre on March 12, 2012. The house fellowship centre started at Marshall d'Avray Hall, located within the University of New Brunswick, Fredericton.

The fellowship initially started with five people and quickly multiplied. This small band of worshippers began attracting attention so much that people thirsty for God learned about this burgeoning fellowship and started attending. On June 1, 2012, Pastor Gbenga Adenuga, then the RCCG area pastor, led some pastors and members from other RCCG parishes in the Atlantic region to officially inaugurate the parish. However, the fellowship witnessed an unexpected decline in attendance shortly after the inauguration, as most attendees stopped attending meetings. Still, the pastor and the faithful brethren steadfastly pressed forward.

The pastor and the members of RCCG Praise Chapel Fredericton embarked on various activities, such as visitations, street evangelism, and a picnic to win souls. These activities resulted in the church's first Sunday service, which was held on September 16, 2012. The church continued meeting at the university for three years until the desire to worship in a more conducive atmosphere resulted in its moving to a more permanent location at 700 McLeod Avenue, Fredericton, where the congregational membership increased.

The journey was fraught with many challenges along the way. Regarding the city's population, there was a shortage of Africans at the time of the parish's inception, which affected its popularity amongst people living in the community. In addition, in the parish's early days, its members were mostly university students, who, at the end of their programs, moved away from Fredericton in search of greener pastures. This demography negatively impacted the growth projections of the church. Additionally, the fact that the city buses did not operate on

Sundays also discouraged people who did not own cars and could not afford to use taxis from attending church services. Since the church was predominantly student-based, finances were a major issue, so the parish had to prioritize what it spent money on. The financial position affected the acquisition of instruments and other needed equipment.

However, despite the many challenges encountered, many souls were saved, and testimonies began to abound because God answered the congregation's prayer requests. This meant that many believers started to be aware of what was happening in Praise Chapel Fredericton. God blessed the church through a brother who donated a minivan to the church in 2015. Having a church vehicle assisted the parish in transporting members to and from church programs. Some of the members in the early days included Brother David Abubakar, Sister Candy Ebimo, Brother Samuel Hanson, Sister Treasure Hanson, Sister Edna Kalu, Sister Funmi Odunsi, Sister Tinu Toki, Brother Seun Akinola, Brother Johnbull Ebonka, and Sister Imaobong Ekwere.

In 2016, Pastor Anthony Iluebbey's family, comprising his wife (Pastor Frances Iluebbey) and their children (Emmanuella, Stephanie, and Jesse), eventually joined him in Canada and provided the much-needed support for the ministry assignment to prosper. Between 2016 and 2019, the church experienced some transformation with the influx of new families to the city. This period saw a departure from the student-based congregation to the emergence of a family-based congregation. As a result, several new units were established, such as the Junior Church and the men's, women's, and youth fellowship groups. The church leadership organized special programs, or "Weekends," around these natural groups, and this produced deeper integration among the members. These fellowships became vehicles for church growth and expansion. The brethren were encouraged to develop their spiritual gifts and leadership abilities during these programs.

The parish organized a Praise concert to boost attendance further, which transformed lives through worship. The concert has become an annual event which attracts a large gathering of people, church choir groups, and anointed music ministers from within Fredericton, other cities in the province of New Brunswick, other Atlantic provinces, and Canada as a whole. This concert has become a blessing indeed.

The Parish Family Weekend is another program inspired by God to celebrate Christian marriages and families. The Lord has used this to sustain and enlarge His work in Fredericton. This annual gathering has evolved into an evangelistic outreach geared towards soul-winning within the city of Fredericton and its environs. Attendance has grown over the years and affords families the much-needed opportunity to have fun during the summer. Many residents of Fredericton look forward to it with enthusiasm.

All Nations Day is another platform that God has used over the years to expand His work in Fredericton. This program celebrates the parish as a multicultural place of worship and a welcoming church. Last year, Praise Chapel Fredericton embarked on a food drive to minister to people in need in our community. To the glory of God, we were able to bless many people and trust that the Lord will sustain this ministry.

As a local parish, Praise Chapel Fredericton has also grown exponentially. Having started with just five members as a fellowship centre back in 2012, we now record an average attendance of over 350 and counting at our Sunday worship services. The parish is undertaking a building project and plans to move to a permanent facility in the not-too-distant future. In addition, the parish's thriving congregation comprises over fifteen nationalities. We also have an online presence, with our services being live-streamed on social media platforms such as YouTube and Facebook. Some members of our congregation have also received spiritual promotion and been ordained as ministers in the Redeemed Christian Church of God.

The church recently moved into another facility at 984 Unit B, Prospect Street, Fredericton. By God's grace, the church services attract people from within the city and from neighbouring towns. A big part of this is due to the fact that we have held dutifully to our mission statement to reach the community with the gospel of Jesus Christ, with an active presence preaching the gospel, inspiring hope, preaching restoration, and spreading the knowledge of our Lord Jesus Christ as the only way to salvation. This we have done to effect changes in our world and have a meaningful impact on people's lives. We trust that the faithful God who has brought us this far will greatly increase us in the future. To God be the glory!

Pastors Anthony and Frances Iluebbey
RCCG Praise Chapel
984 Prospect Street, Fredericton NB E3B 2T8
Phone: (506) 262-5614
www.rccgpcf.org

RCCG JOY IN THE MORNING, ST. JOHN'S NEWFOUNDLAND AND LABRADOR

A vision came one night to Pastor Emeka Mba Ezera during the annual worker's meeting in July 2012 at the Redemption Camp in Nigeria. The vision was to relocate RCCG to Northeastern Canada, precisely where the trees are lively with branches but without leaves on them and a dairy cow is tied to a tree. That was the content of the vision of the place. God started the Journey. A Canadian citizen from Newfoundland eventually came to Nigeria to marry his daughter, and the wedding was conducted in RCCG Gethsemane Parish in Lagos Province 25, Gatewa, in June 2013. A house fellowship started in the daughter's house (104 North Pond Road, St. John's) in November 2014.

Pastor Emeka and Pastor Mrs. Nnena Ezera, the pastors in charge of All Time Triumphant Parish LP25 area, traveled to Newfoundland on Parent and Grandparent Super Visa arrangements. Being aware of the vision, Pastor Nnena carried with her the RCCG logo and banner, an attendance register, Believers' Class manuals, Workers in Training manuals, Sunday School manuals, Digging Deep manuals, Faith Clinic manuals, and an official RCCG stamp. On arrival in St. John's, Newfoundland, she observed no established RCCG Church in the province of Newfoundland and Labrador.

On Sunday, June 7, 2015, RCCG Joy in the Morning was officially inaugurated by Pastor Debo Akande, Pastor in Charge of Lagos Province 25. Incidentally, Pastor E.A. Adeboye was in Canada in June 2015; he was duly informed of the newly planted RCCG Church in Newfoundland. In order to hold the church, Pastor Nnena decided to return to school at Memorial University of Newfoundland and apply for a study permit visa in the process. Accordingly, Pastor Emeka Ezera supported his wife on the church planting mission while he remained on the Super Visa arrangements. GOD, who is the owner of the church, has been faithful. He made available the following foundation members: the Ezera family, the Enahoro family, the Jenrola family, the Chilaka family, Nora Kelechi, Augustin Osarogiagbon, Chinyere Uwambe, Yinka Aiyeonegun, Philomena Ohio Kolawole, Emmanuel Anyaeto, Kayode Dairo, and Brenda Omahli. There have been man-made spiritual challenges and stumbling blocks, but we are undaunted and are not moved by them. We are confident that the church came by revelation and not influenced by man. God alone has been the only source and supplier of the needs of the church.

Pastor Emeka Mba Ezera and Pastor Mrs. Nnena E. Ezera
RCCG Joy in the Morning
MUN-CHAPEL: 240 Prince Philip Drive, St. John's, NL A1B 3R5
MAILING ADDRESS: 3 New Pennywell Road #305, St. John's NL A1B 4E4
Phone: (709) 765-3458; (709) 986-6224

RCCG DOMINION SANCTUARY DARTMOUTH, NOVA SCOTIA

Dominion Sanctuary Dartmouth, a parish of the Redeemed Christian Church of God (RCCG), was planted on September 16, 2018. Our mother church is Restoration Chapel Halifax, under the leadership of Pastors Simeon and Juliet Olugbile, with the support of the following families as foundation members: the Adedejis, the Obisesans, the Baloguns, the Emekas, the Mishiacks, the Efunkoyas, and other youth volunteers who form the youth church at RCCG Restoration Chapel. Our first service was held at the Hearthstone Inn, 313 Prince Albert Road, Dartmouth, NS B2Y 1N3.

After six months of groundbreaking work, afternoon services, evangelism across Dartmouth, and prayers, the church moved into a permanent venue at 169 Main Street, Dartmouth, for our inaugural service. We were honoured to host our provincial pastor, Pastor Gbenga Adenuga; our zonal pastors, Simeon and Juliet Olugbile; and Pastor Gladys Omamofe, who commissioned the pioneering pastors, Dayo and Aanu Adedeji. Dominion Sanctuary held its inaugural service on February 24, 2019. The duo of pastors brought with them an unwavering passion for God and people, commitment, and a shared vision to create a vibrant spiritual home for the community.

In the Main Street community, Dominion Sanctuary transcended its role as a mere place of worship; it became a vibrant community hub where relationships were formed, spiritual encounters were experienced, and lasting bonds of friendship were forged.

From its humble beginnings, Dominion Sanctuary experienced rapid growth, attracting members from diverse backgrounds, including students, families, and newcomers to Canada. The journey was not without its challenges. The church faced difficulties in securing suitable space for gatherings, grappling with escalating rent costs and venue limitations. Despite these obstacles, the congregation remained steadfast in their faith, believing God would provide a permanent home for their worship.

As a church comprising predominantly immigrant members, Dominion Sanctuary played a vital role in providing support and guidance to newcomers adjusting to life in Dartmouth. Through practical assistance, mentorship programs, and integration initiatives, the church became a beacon of hope and belonging for immigrants and international students seeking community and connection.

As Dominion Sanctuary continued to grow, testimonies began to emerge, showcasing the transformative power of faith and fellowship within the community. Members shared stories of answered prayers, miraculous interventions, and life-changing encounters with God. The church's emphasis on prayer, worship, and spiritual nourishment created a sacred space where individuals found healing, belonging, and purpose.

Over time, Dominion Sanctuary implemented various special programs and outreach initiatives to meet the diverse needs of its members and the broader community. These initiatives have included:

- The annual Easter Let's-Go-A-Fishing outreach
- The summer family barbecue and community outreach
- The hosting of Prayer Room, an online prayer community, fostering deeper spiritual connections and collective intercession
- The establishment of settlement programs and support services for immigrants, offering vital assistance with integration, housing, employment, and mentorship
- Children's enrichment classes and online Bible studies, nurturing the spiritual growth of young members and equipping them for their journey of faith
- Welfare initiatives aimed at caring for the community, including food drives, outreach events, and support for those in need

After we had endured numerous challenges, God blessed Dominion Sanctuary recently with a temporary but stable place of worship at 21 Woodlawn Street, Dartmouth. This providential provision brought a sense of stability and continuity to the congregation, allowing them to gather in a dedicated space to worship, pray, and find fellowship together.

Considering our tremendous growth, it has become imperative for us to secure a larger space that can comfortably accommodate the diverse ministerial needs and activities of our church. After an extensive search, we found a remarkable church-building property located at 50 Ritcey Crescent, Dartmouth, Nova Scotia. The five-acre lot features a purpose-built church with space for a church auditorium, three large offices, six classrooms for the children's church and creche center, and a large kitchen with a hall for events and a Youth Hall. This facility would serve as an exceptional sanctuary, a place of worship, a Dominion Kids and Youth Centre, and a vibrant hub for community engagement and kingdom expansion. To realize this transformative opportunity, we have successfully negotiated to purchase the property for $1,100,000. However, according to feedback from commercial mortgage brokers and bankers, to proceed with the purchase we need to raise a 30% to 35% ($330,000 to $385,000) down payment. The church community has been able to raise $250,000, or 22.7% of the purchase price, towards the down payment, and we trust the Lord for the completion of the project.

As Dominion Sanctuary Dartmouth continues its journey of faith and service, it remains dedicated to spreading the message of God's love and transforming power within the community. By the grace of God, with an unwavering commitment to prayer, worship, and outreach, the church stands poised to make an even greater impact in the years ahead.

Pastors Oludayo and Aanu Adedeji
RCCG Dominion Sanctuary
21 Woodlawn Road, Dartmouth, NS B2W 2R6
Phone: (902) 222-0716
www.dominionsanctuary.ca

RCCG CITY OF DAVID, SYDNEY, NOVA SCOTIA

RCCG City of David started in Sydney, Cape Breton, in March 2020. The parish was pioneered with support from Pastor Gbenga Adenuga, now provincial pastor; Pastor Gladys Omamofe, now zonal pastor; and RCCG Jesus House Halifax. City of David had its first service on March 8, 2020, at the Holiday Inn in Sydney.

In September 2020, the parish moved to another location, and the Lord kept adding to the number of congregants. There were complaints from the landlord about "too much Jesus" in the building, and people also petitioned to keep the building from "being converted to a church." Therefore, the church moved again in October 2021 to another building. The congregation grew from twenty or thirty members to over a hundred worshippers every Sunday. This resulted in the new space becoming extremely inadequate for the membership. In February 2023, the parish moved to its current location: 480 Kings Road, Sydney, NS B1S 1A8.

The pioneering pastor was Pastor Psalmuel Akinbiyi Bibilari, who was assisted by pioneering members Brother Peter Oyedijo, Sister Esther Alu, Sister Barbara Amurun, Brother Yemi Oyeleye, and Brother Femi Adeshina. The church held services at the Holiday Inn from March to August 2020, and other members came along to join, notably Sister Teni Awosusi and her three children: Josh, Mathilda, and Mabel. Pastor Bibilari, his wife, AnuOluwa, and their sons Olatide and Olatoye relocated from Nigeria and joined the church in September 2022.

Presently, there are about 250 worshippers at City of David. Regular worship meetings include Sunday Family Worship at 10:30 am, Sunday School at 9:45 am, Tuesday Bible Study at 6:30 pm, and Friday Prayer Meeting at 6:30 pm. In addition, the church organizes spiritual and community engagement programs, such as Engage Sydney, Breakfast With Jesus, Walk for Life (Jesus), After School for Children, and our yearly conference, Festival of the Light. By the grace of God, and with permission from the zone and province, City of David planted a parish in Glace Bay, about twenty-five minutes' drive from Sydney, and that church is thriving.

Pastor Psalmuel Akinbiyi Bibilari
RCCG City of David
480 Kings Road, Sydney, Nova Scotia B1S 1A8
Phone: (902) 919-4497
www.rccgcods.org

RCCG OPEN DOOR SANCTUARY, TRURO, NOVA SCOTIA

Truro is a town in Nova Scotia that was once known as the centre of revival. The beautiful town is known as the hub of Nova Scotia because it is at the geographic center of the province. Likewise, it has been at the center of God's agenda to have a parish of the Redeemed Christian Church of God (RCCG). This town is about an hour's drive from Halifax, where the next closest parish of the church is located.

For many years, about three families—the Oshikoyas, the Akinsikus, and the Esans (with the Adebowale family, who joined them immediately after the pandemic)—drove an hour every Sunday to fellowship at RCCG parishes in Halifax. In the fullness of time, God laid it in the heart of Pastors Simon and Juliet Fagbile (current Pastors in charge of Atlantic Zone 2) to start the work in Truro. This had been a longtime vision in their hearts since at least 2016. The work began with a little seed in the ground through daily prayer walks around the town and many spiritual mappings.

Many attempts were made to start the work fully pre-COVID, but when the time came, God opened the door of favour to Truro. He sent some more families, students, and professionals to the land and put in their hearts a willingness and desire to start the work in Truro. By divine connection and by His own power, God connected all of us with Pastor and Pastor Mrs. Fagbile, and Grace was made available to start. The church started with an online fellowship over Zoom before transitioning into a physical meeting. We met at the community center and at St. David United's church hall before relocating to our current location at 266 Pictou Road in Bible Hill. God made financial provisions for establishing the physical church, rental, and equipment gracefully through RCCG Restoration Sanctuary Halifax and several individuals.

On July 10, 2022, RCCG Open Door Sanctuary held its first service at its current location. In support of the new church, the brethren from RCCG Restoration Sanctuary Halifax organized an evangelic outreach themed "Light Up Truro" on July 24, 2022, at Victoria Park in Truro. God has been faithful; He has increased His church on every side.

This first service was officiated by Pastors Simeon and Juliet Fagbile and a number of delegates from RCCG Restoration Chapel Halifax. The pioneer and current pastors are Pastors Seun and Korede Esan; they have been supported by other ministers and workers as well. We have a vision to impact our land with the grace and love of Christ; however, our major challenge is finding a befitting place of worship.

Pastors Seun and Korede Esan
RCCG Open Door Sanctuary
266B Pictou Rd, Truro–Bible Hill, NS B2N 2T3
Phone: (902) 305-4121
www.rccgods.ca

RCCG KING'S COURT ST. JOHN'S NEWFOUNDLAND AND LABRADOR

The Redeemed Christian Church of God King's Court parish was founded on November 17, 2023, by Pastor Akintola Sunday and Akintola Odunola in the city of St. John's, Newfoundland and Labrador, under RCCG ACT-1, Atlantic Province 3. At the inception, the mother church was RCCG Victory Centre in Rochester, New York, led by Pastor and Pastor Mrs. Aaron Olaosebikan.

Initially, it was very difficult to find a space, but eventually, we got a rented hall. After a couple of Sundays, we were asked to leave due to "noise disturbances," which they said were against their policy. There was no way we could run a church service without praising and worshiping God and praying, so we were forced to leave. However, God, in His infinite mercy, made a way for us, and in December 2023, we were able to secure another location at a Holiday Inn. We continue to hold our services there, and the church has been growing in numbers and in capacity, both spiritually and physically, to the glory of God. In March 2024, we welcomed a bouncing baby boy. To God Be All the Glory.

Pastors Sunday and Odunola Akintola
RCCG King's Court
180 Portugal Cove Road, St. John's NL A1B 2N2
Phone: (709) 219-2876 or (709) 763-9627
www.rccgkingscourtnl.org

RCCG GREAT GRACE, GLACE BAY, NOVA SCOTIA

RCCG Great Grace, located in Glace Bay on Cape Breton Island, Nova Scotia, was birthed by RCCG City of David (COD) in Sydney. It had its inaugural service on December 3, 2023, and its first full Sunday service on December 10, 2023, with forty-two members in attendance. The inaugural service was graced by the parish pastor of COD, Pastor Psalmuel Bibilari (representing Pastor Gladys, the zonal pastor); Pastor Psalmuel's wife, Pastor Mrs. Anne Bibilari; and the ministers and some members of COD.

The church began in October 2023 with two house fellowship centers that met every Sunday evening, with a total of twenty members. The house fellowships continued for about two months until the church was able to secure a worship center (a rented hall), and the inauguration was conducted on December 3, 2023. Space and transportation of members to church became issues almost immediately because the church witnessed drastic growth, being the first Nigerian church and in fact the first black church in Glace Bay. Glory to God!

The inception of the church was an answered prayer, allowing brethren who couldn't travel thirty minutes or more to the church in Sydney to gather and worship God. At this point, the membership represented a mixture of several cultural backgrounds and ethnicities, which also resulted in some adjustments in the general style of worship, with the aim of retaining members of other communities such as Indian and Canadian.

As more members joined and the church continued to grow, the need arose for the church to search for a permanent and larger space. The recent move to our current location at 151 Commercial Street in Glace Bay has filled this need. The transportation challenge is still an issue, but God is helping His church as some members are also supporting the parish pastor in offering transportation to members, and God continues to strengthen and add to His church.

The workers and ministers at RCCG Great Grace Glace Bay are:

- Kayode Olaleye, pastor in charge
- Bukola Lawal-Olaleye, wife of the pastor in charge:
- Four altar ministers
- Eleven unit coordinators
- Twenty kingdom workers

We thank God for his faithfulness as we continue to trust him for the promise of DIVINE LIFTING in this year 2024. Praise the Lord! Hallelujah!!

Pastors Kayode and Bukola Olaleye
RCCG Great Grace, Glace Bay, Nova Scotia
151 Commercial Street, Glace Bay, NS B1A 3B9
Phone: (782) 503-0411

RCCG COMMUNAUTÉ DE LA COMPASSION, SHEDIAC, NEW BRUNSWICK

Our history started in November 2023; my wife and I were called by Pastors Gbenga and Bisi Adenuga, Pastors in Charge of Atlantic 1 Province, after the evening prayer meeting. In that meeting, we were informed about the new direction the church was going to take, especially in matters of church planting. Pastors Gbenga and Bisi Adenuga advised us that, knowing our heart for ministry, they wanted to discuss with us the possibility of church planting in one of the cities in New Brunswick. We were encouraged to think about that option with the understanding that we would have the freedom to stay and continue to be part of Cornerstone Chapel Moncton if we preferred. My wife (Beatrice Boungou) answered that this question of going to plant a church was an answer to a prayer. We asked for the blessings of our provincial pastors as we agreed to go and start a new parish. We were then informed that the new parish had to be at least fifteen minutes' drive from any existing RCCG parish, in this case, Cornerstone Chapel Moncton. My wife and I decided to pray and to visit several cities: Amherst, Sackville, Sussex, and Shediac. Shediac was the last city we visited. As we crossed the bridge and entered the city, we both felt at peace and concluded that Shediac was the city to which God was leading us to pioneer a church.

On December 8, 2023, we visited our provincial pastors to report about the choice of the city and find out if Shediac's location would meet the RCCG's church-planting criteria. Shediac was approved as the location of the RCCG's new parish. Then followed a conversation about the next steps. My wife and I wanted to learn something that would be beneficial for us. We asked Pastors Gbenga and Bisi Adenuga about their journey in establishing Cornerstone Chapel Moncton. At the end, we were told they would be available any time we had questions about ministry.

In naming the church in Shediac, we felt inspired by the compassion of Jesus Christ as recorded in the scriptures in Matthew 9:35–38. We were brought to the realization that we wanted to have a community that exhibited the Heart of Jesus, so we decided to call the new church parish Communauté de la Compassion, Shediac. Communauté de la Compassion RCCG, Shediac was registered on January 19, 2024.

The founding members were:

- Pastors Gbenga and Bisi Adenuga
- Aristide and Beatrice Boungou

The first directors for the registration were:

- Aristide Boungou
- Beatrice Boungou
- Simplice Baleckita

The first church service was held at Seely's Motel in Shediac on February 25, 2024, at 3:30 pm. My wife and I were anointed as pastors of the new parish by Pastors Gbenga and Bisi Adenuga.

Finding a core group to build the new community has been a challenge, as no other family came with us on this assignment. Work has started—we thank Cornerstone Chapel Moncton for their support in this journey. May God take all the Glory.

Pastors Aristide and Beatrice Boungou
Communauté de la Compassion RCCG, Shediac
CP 9068, Shediac PO Main NB E4P 8W5
Phone: (506) 588-7802

RCCG VICTORY SANCTUARY, NEW MINAS, NOVA SCOTIA

RCCG Victory Sanctuary was planted after several years of spiritual mapping, community engagement, and periodic visits during vacations, celebrations, graduation, and other festive periods, such as Apple Blossom festivals in the valley. The church planting initiative was undertaken under the supervision of Pastor Simeon Fagbile and his wife, who were instrumental in our church's establishment. Pastor Simeon Fagbile and his family had first settled in the valley, but because of a lack of manpower, he could not achieve his desired dream. The house fellowship started by their daughter at Acadia University was not functional due to a lack of commitment on the part of the members.

However, in the spring of 2021, Pastor Simeon Fagbile met my wife, Dr. Mrs. Toyin Adewumi, who had relocated from South Africa (RCCG Rivers of Joy) and was undertaking an academic program at Acadia University. This was the beginning of the idea that we could be the arrowhead of the program if Dr. Mrs. Adewumi's spouse would relocate to Canada. One year later, the husband arrived in Canada and began ministerial service, initially as the leader of the outreach and evangelism department of RCCG Restoration Chapel Halifax under Pastor Fagbile's mentorship.

The Valley municipality oscillated among three townships—Wolfville, New Minas, and Kentville—and the possibility of access by these three dominant townships. Deciding on a church venue and location was challenging because these three townships had different demographics and characteristics. Wolfville is the seat of youth because of Acadia University, our target population. New Minas is the commercial hub and predominantly residential for most town dwellers. Kentville is the seat of government and predominantly those in public service. A choice was made to situate the church in centrally located New Minas for easier accessibility by residents of all three townships. We are grateful for the leadership of the women's ministry of RCCG Restoration Chapel Halifax. They made several trips to be involved in various community social responsibility programs in Wolfville, Nova Scotia. All these efforts finally paid off, and we are grateful for their continued contributions and support.

The church started on Sunday, January 21, 2024. The Lord has given us a building facility with about 5,000 square feet of floor space. The following are our founding members: Lawrence Adewumi (Pastor in Charge), Pastor Olusegun Olusipe, Oluwatoyin Adewumi, the Shodunke family, Ike Imegwu, Olayinka Fatimileyin, Anthony Fadoro, Olamide Israel, Alicia Ekiemabor, and Victoria Mukoro. This is our journey so far. Thank you.

Pastors Lawrence & Toyin Adewumi
RCCG Victory Sanctuary
68 Crescent Drive, New Minas NS
Phone: (902) 399 6578 or (782) 641 2601

RCCG THRONE OF GRACE, GANDER, NEWFOUNDLAND

We were ordained Pastor and Assistant Pastor in the RCCG in Ireland. Our family relocated from the Republic of Ireland to Newfoundland, Canada, in August 2018 due to our professional careers. Prior to this, we had served at RCCG Open Heavens in Ireland. We settled in the town of Gander, Newfoundland, and we soon discovered that the nearest RCCG church was about 330 km away from us, and hence, we could afford to attend Sunday service at the RCCG church only a few times a year! This was very tough for us. We later joined a nearby Pentecostal church, but the experience was not the same as our RCCG church.

In October 2022, we noticed more people coming into the city of Gander to settle, and we subsequently rallied ourselves together by doing weekly Bible study. Our Bible study group gained momentum and became a source of blessing to our members. We were able to connect and meet our needs. Eventually the RCCG Throne of Grace parish evolved from the Bible study group that started with two families and two youths.

Our inaugural service was held on March 17, 2024, using space in one of our local hotels. Eleven adults and three children attended.

Our founding members were Pastors Orefuwa and family, Mr. and Mrs. Adeneye and family, Miss Tinuola Orebanjo, and Mr. Kingsley Okai.

We are trusting God for His work to continue to prosper in our city and environment, and our current challenges will soon become a testimony in Jesus' name. Amen.

Dr. Felix Orefuwa and Dr. Mrs. Olusola Orefuwa
RCCG Throne of Grace
Quality Hotels and Suites, 100 Trans-Canada Highway
Gander, NL A1V 1P5
Phone: (709) 422-4134

Provincial Headquarters, Cornerstone Chapel Moncton

(2008) First Baby Dedication at Jesus House Halifax

(May 10, 2009) Mother's Day at Cornerstone Chapel Moncton

(May 10, 2009) Mother's Day at Cornerstone Chapel Moncton

(2009) Inauguration Weekend Invitation, Cornerstone Chapel Moncton

(May 23, 2009) Inauguration Saturday at Cornerstone Chapel Moncton with Tofunmi Adenuga (Six-year-old) and Premier Brian Gallant

(May 24, 2009) Inauguration Service at Cornerstone Chapel Moncton

(May 24, 2009) Inauguration Day at Cornerstone Chapel Moncton, Pastor Paul (Glad Tidings Church)

(May 24, 2009) Inauguration Day at Cornerstone Chapel Moncton.
From Left: Pastor Femi Olawale, Pastors Gbenga
and Bisi Adenuga, and Pastor Yinka Dada

(May 24, 2009) Inauguration Day at Cornerstone Chapel Moncton

(May 24, 2009) Inauguration Day at Cornerstone Chapel Moncton. From Left: Beatrice and Aristide Boungou, Pastor Paul, and Pastors Gbenga and Bisi Adenuga

(May 24, 2009) Pastor Yinka Dada and Pastor Femi Olawale

(May 24, 2009) Pastors Gbenga and Bisi Adenuga

(2012) Inauguration Service, Pavilion of Redemption Saint John NB

(2013) Inauguration Service, Praise Chapel Fredericton.
From Left: Pastor Bisi Adenuga, Pastor John Adegbengo, Pastor Anthony Iluebbey, Pastor Gladys Omamofe, and Pastor Gbenga Adenuga

(2014) FIFA U-20 Women's World Cup Nigerian Team

(2014) First Anniversary, Living Word Assembly PEI.
From Left: Dr. Tunde Apantaku, Tofunmi Apantaku (One-year-old), Sis. Bunmi Apantaku, and Nifemi Apantaku (10-year-old) with Pastors Abiodun and Yemi Olusoji (The Pioneering Pastors)

(2014) First Anniversary, Living Word Assembly PEI

(2015) Third Anniversary, Pavilion of Redemption Saint John. From Left: Pastor Tunde Babalola (RCCG Republic of Ireland) with Pastors Felicia and John Adegbenjo (The Pioneer Pastors)

(Canada Day 2017) Moncton Mayor Dawn Arnold at Cornerstone Chapel Moncton

(2018) Fifth Anniversary, Praise Chapel Fredericton

(2018) Pastors Anthony and Frances Iluebbey
and Others at Praise Chapel Fredericton

Corporate Social Responsibility Initiative at Praise Chapel Fredericton

(2018) Mother's Day at Cornerstone Chapel Moncton

(2018) Mother's Day at Mount Zion St. John's NL

(2018) Pastor Simeon Fagbile Receiving a Community Recognition Award from the Nova Scotia House of Assembly

HISTORY OF RCCG IN ATLANTIC CANADA

(2022) Tenth Anniversary, Pavilion of Redemption Saint John NB

(2022) Women's Conference at Mount Zion St. John's NL

(2023) Inauguration Service, Great Grace Gracie NS

(2023) Inauguration Service, Kings Court St. John's NL

(2023) Provincial Pastors' Visit to Open Door Sanctuary Truro with Pastors Seun and Korede Esan

(2024) Inauguration Service, Communauté de la Compassion Shediac

Provincial Pastor Visit to Open Door Sanctuary Truro.
Left to Right: Pastor and Pastor Mrs. Fagbile, Pastor and Pastor Mrs. Esan (Parish Pastor), Pastor and Pastor Mrs. Adenuga, Pastor and Pastor Mrs. Adedeji, and Dr. Patrick Oniah.

Open Door Sanctuary Truro Visit to Member of Parliament for the Riding of Cumberland—Colchester Office.
Left to Right: Mr. Mohammed Oshikoya, Pastor Olubunmi Adebowale, Pastor Seun Esan, Member of Parliament Dr. Stephen Ellis, Pastor Korede Esan, Shindara Esan, Dr. Moji Oniah, and Mrs. Cadine Foster.

CHAPTER SIX

Our Statement of Faith

But without faith it is impossible to please Him, for he who comes to God must believe that He is, and that He is a rewarder of those who diligently seek Him.
—Hebrews 11:6

WE BELIEVE IN:

THE BIBLE
We believe that the Bible is God's Word. The truth revealed in it did not have its origin with men, but with God. The Holy Spirit inspired the human authors of the Bible. Its central theme and purpose is the salvation of man (2 Timothy 3:16–17; 2 Peter 1:20–21).

GOD
As revealed unto us by the Bible, we believe that there is only one God (Isaiah 43:10–11; John 1:1–3).

JESUS CHRIST
Jesus of Nazareth is the Christ, the Son of the living God. He has existed throughout eternity, one of the persons of the Holy Trinity. According to the scriptures, Jesus Christ came to the world purposely to save sinners (John 1:1–14; Hebrews 4:14–15).

THE HOLY SPIRIT

The Holy Spirit is the third Person in the TRINITY. He has the same power, the same glory with God the Father and God the Son. He performs the work of regeneration for man (John 3:5–6; John 15:26).

THE TRINITY

We believe in the Divine Trinity. One Triune God exists in three Persons—Father, Son, and Holy Spirit—eternal in being, identical in nature, equal in power and glory, and having the same attributes and perfections (2 Corinthians 13:14; 1 John 5:7).

THE FALL OF MAN

Man (Adam) was created in the image of God before whom he walked in innocence, holiness, and purity, but by voluntary disobedience and transgression, he fell from the glory of God to the depths of sin. In his fallen state, man is incapable of pleasing God or having any relationship with Him (Genesis 1:26–31; Romans 5:12–21).

SALVATION

Jesus Christ came to save us from our sins. Himself without sin, He took our sins upon Him. To appropriate salvation, we must acknowledge our sins and repent from them; we must believe that Christ died for us and rose again; we must receive the risen Christ as our personal Saviour, and we must publicly confess Him as our Lord, that we might be forgiven and receive eternal life (Romans 10:8–13).

SANCTIFICATION

The word for sanctification in the Greek language is *hagiasmos*, meaning (1) to be apart from sin or (2) consecrated unto God. It is the total yielding of one's life to the Holy Spirit: living the crucified life, being an overcomer, and being conformed to the image of Christ Himself. Perfection and true holiness are impossible without the indwelling of the Holy Spirit (1 Peter 1:15–17).

BAPTISM OF THE HOLY SPIRIT

Baptism in the Holy Ghost is a supernatural endowment with power from heaven to equip the Christian for effective witness and service. It enables the Christian to build up his own spiritual life by direct and continual communion with God and is the gateway into a life in which both the gifts and fruits of the Holy Ghost should be manifested (Acts 2:38–39).

DIVINE HEALING

Sickness is a direct consequence of the fall of man and his continuance in sin. Healing for our bodies from God comes to us through appropriation of the finished work of Christ on the cross of Calvary by faith in the word of God and the manifestation of the gift of healing (Isaiah 53:5–10).

THE RAPTURE OF THE CHURCH

The rapture describes an event in the future when Jesus Christ will, in the twinkling of an eye, change all believers (living and dead) to immortal, giving them a resurrected body and catching them up to meet the Lord in the air (1 Corinthians 15:23, 51–58).

THE GREAT TRIBULATION

This is a seven-year span of future world history of the reign of antichrist following immediately after the rapture: It will be the darkest time the world has ever known. Man's cup of iniquity is filled to overflowing, and God brings judgment upon the earth for man's rejection of His son (Revelation 19).

THE MILLENNIAL REIGN OF JESUS CHRIST
The millennial age is a period of one thousand years in which the purpose of God is fully realized on the earth. It will be a time of theocratic kingdom—a time of peace, joy, holiness, glory, comfort, justice, full knowledge, and the removal of curse and sickness. This period will come after the seven years' reign of antichrist (Revelation 20:1–15).

THE JUDGEMENT SEAT OF CHRIST
The judgment seat of Christ is the judgment of believers. It is not a judgment of condemnation but a judgment of reward, where believers will be rewarded according to our faithfulness in our service to God, the quality of our Christian walk, and the use of our God-given gifts and talents (2 Corinthians 5:10).

THE ETERNAL HEAVEN
The present earth that is so marred and cursed by Satan's evil will pass away after the Great White Throne Judgment. After the dissolution of the present (atmospheric) heaven and earth at the end of the one thousand years (the millennium), God will create a new heaven and a new earth better than anything this world has ever known. The new earth will be the Christian heaven. It is the glorious eternal home of born-again believers (Revelation 21:1–5; Revelation 22:1–5).

ETERNAL LAKE OF FIRE (HELL)
The lake of fire (commonly called hell) is the final abode of Satan and those sinners who reject Jesus as their Lord and saviour (Luke 16:19–31; Revelations 20:10,15).

WATER BAPTISM

Baptism in water is an outward act of obedience, by which we testify of the change of believing in Christ that has taken place in our hearts. By this act, we make ourselves one with Christ in His burial and in His resurrection (Acts 2:38–41).

RESTITUTION

Restitution is the act of restoring anything to its rightful owner or the act of giving an equivalent for loss or damage. This is to be done whether the person injured knew it or not—God knows (Acts 24:16).

Note: Restitution that would implicate others or bring injury or harm to others needs to be undertaken with care and God's wisdom. In such cases, it is necessary to seek counselling from a faithful, experienced, competent, mature Christian teacher and preacher (who, of course, believes and teaches "the whole counsel of God").

THE LORD'S SUPPER

The Lord's Supper, consisting of the elements—bread and the fruit of the vine—is the symbol expressing our sharing the divine nature of our Lord Jesus Christ. It is a memorial of His suffering and death and a prophecy of His second coming. Jesus Christ commanded the church to do it in His remembrance (Luke 22:14–19; 1 Corinthians 11:26).

Our Values

Finally, brethren, whatever things are true, whatever things are noble, whatever things are just, whatever things are pure, whatever things are lovely, whatever things are of good report, if there is any virtue and if there is anything praiseworthy—meditate on these things.
—Philippians 4:8

We Value the Pursuit of God—to know more of Him through private and public worship.

We Value Christlikeness—to minister by serving people the way He did with compassion, under the power and anointing of the Holy Spirit.

We Value Godly Family Life—to cultivate an environment in which the spiritual, emotional and social growth of the future generations can be fully accomplished.

We Value Marital Fidelity—where husband and wife can depend on each other to provide spiritual, emotional, and intimate needs.

We Value Purposeful Singleness—where the uniqueness of being single (unmarried) should be used to bless the church.

We Value the Church of God as the Body of Christ—seeking its good, growth, and prosperity.

We Value the Individual Members of the Church—to help members to grow in the grace and to fully realize their God-given potentials.

We Value Servant Leadership— to serve members of the church as Christ did, selflessly, and not for profit or self-glorification.

We Value the Mercy of God—to extend mercy to another and to all who come under the ministry of the church.

We Value Giving—recognizing in humility that all the goodness we receive from God is a result of His mercies, even those blessings we may regard as "rights," because of our relationship with Him as children.

We Value Personal and Corporate Integrity—to conduct our affairs truthfully and honestly such that the gospel of Jesus Christ shall not suffer any reproach because of our conduct.

We Love Unity in the Body of Christ—we believe in Jesus Christ as Lord and Saviour, belong to one body of Christ, and seek to maintain unity with all such believers.

We Value Simplicity—to do nothing in our private and public worship just for "effects" and "showing off."

We Value Modesty in Our Lifestyle—to be generous and gracious in our speech, firm in our convictions, and chaste in our dressing.

Matthew 5:16 reads: "In the same way, let your light shine before others, that they may see your good deeds and glorify your Father in heaven." This instruction (command) of our Lord Jesus Christ emphasizes the importance of being a positive influence in the world and living out one's faith through actions that reflect God's love and character. Accordingly, these statements of faith and values outline beliefs, principles, and convictions held by every member of the Redeemed Christian Church of God (RCCG) worldwide. They serve as guiding principles for our decision-making, behavior, and interactions within any community in which we happen to find ourselves. These values ultimately guide our actions and relationships in shaping our collective journey towards a more compassionate, just, and righteous lifestyle in this present world. Considering these, we remain committed to living out our faith and values with integrity, compassion, and a desire to glorify God in all that we do.

Incorporating these statements of faith and values into our work and lives helps provide a framework for personal lifestyle guidance that aligns with our corporate beliefs. Here is how you might use it:

1. **Work Ethic**: In your professional endeavors, you would strive to uphold the values of integrity, honesty, and excellence, ensuring that your actions and decisions reflect your commitment to Christian principles.
2. **Ethical Decision-Making**: When faced with ethical dilemmas, you would refer to your statement of faith and values to guide your choices, seeking to honor God and serve others in your decision-making process.
3. **Interpersonal Relationships**: In your interactions with colleagues, clients, and stakeholders, you would demonstrate compassion, respect, and humility, recognizing the dignity and worth of everyone as created in the image of God.
4. **Service and Outreach**: You would actively engage in acts of service and outreach, both within your professional context and in your personal lives, seeking to share the love of Christ and meet the needs of others in practical ways.
5. **Personal Growth and Discipleship**: You would prioritize personal growth in your faith, pursuing spiritual disciplines such as prayer, Bible study, and fellowship with other believers, while also seeking opportunities for discipleship and mentorship.
6. **Advocacy and Justice**: You would advocate for justice and righteousness in your spheres of influence, standing up against injustice, oppression, and inequality, and working towards positive change in alignment with God's kingdom values.
7. **Mission and Evangelism**: You would see your secular work and personal lives as opportunities for mission and evangelism, sharing

the gospel through both your words and your actions, and seeking to make disciples of all nations as commanded by Jesus Christ.

Overall, integrating these statements of faith and values into your day-to-day lives provides a holistic approach to living out your Christian faith, impacting both your professional endeavors and your personal relationships in a meaningful and purposeful way.

CHAPTER SEVEN

RCCG Atlantic Canada Conference Profile

Now, brethren, concerning the coming of our Lord Jesus Christ and our gathering together to Him, we ask you, not to be soon shaken in mind or troubled, either by spirit or by word or by letter, as if from us, as though the day of Christ had come.
—2 Thessalonians 2:1–2

Each year since 2009, the Atlantic Canada AT1 Conference has been held the weekend preceding the 25th day of May.

Dates: **May 22–24, 2009**
Name: Cornerstone Inauguration
Theme: **A New Dawn**
Venue: Cornerstone Chapel Moncton (CCM)
Speakers: Pastors Femi Olawale and Yinka Dada

Dates: **May 21–22, 2010**
Name: Atlantic Youth and Young Adults Retreat
Theme: **To Be the Best**
Venue: Cornerstone Chapel Moncton (CCM)
Speakers: Pastor Gbenga Adenuga

Dates: **May 20–22, 2011**
Name: Atlantic Youth and Young Adults Conference
Theme: **Born To Lead**
Venue: Cornerstone Chapel Moncton (CCM)
Speakers: Pastor Gbenga and Bisi Adenuga

Dates: **May 18–20, 2012**
Name: Atlantic Area Workers Conference
Theme: **You Can Choose Your Destiny**
Venue: Cornerstone Chapel Moncton (CCM)
Speakers: Pastors Olu Ayeni and Gbenga and Bisi Adenuga

Dates: **May 17–19, 2013**
Name: Atlantic Area Conference
Theme: **Thriving in Stormy Seasons**
Venue: Cornerstone Chapel Moncton (CCM)
Speakers: Pastors Olu Ayeni and Gbenga Adenuga

Dates: **May 16–18, 2014**
Name: Zonal Conference/Provincial Pastor's visit
Theme: **Divine Impact**
Venue: Cornerstone Chapel Moncton (CCM)
Speakers: Pastors Yinka and Toyin Dada and Rev. Bode Akindele

Dates: **May 15–17, 2015**
Name: Zonal Conference/Provincial Pastor's visit
Theme: **Change**
Venue: Cornerstone Chapel Moncton (CCM)
Speakers: Pastors Yinka and Toyin Dada

Dates: **May 20–21, 2016**
Name: Zonal Conference/Provincial Pastor's visit
Theme: **Enlarge**
Venue: Crandall University Moncton
Speakers: Rev. George Adegboye and Pastor Yinka Dada

Dates: **July 27 - 30, 2017**
Name: Young Adults and Singles Ministry
Theme: **Live It Loud**
Venue: Mount Allison University (MtA) Sackville
Speakers: Pastors Dare Adeboye, Femi Olawale, and Tayo Ojajuni

Dates: **May 17–19, 2018**
Name: Zonal Conference/Provincial Pastor's visit
Theme: **Victory**
Venue: Université de Moncton
Speakers: Rev. George Adegboye, Pastors Tayo Ojajuni and Seun Jonathan

Dates: **May 17–19, 2019**
Name: Zonal Conference/Provincial Pastor's visit
Theme: **Rehoboth**
Venue: Pavilion of Redemption, Saint John, New Brunswick
Speakers: Pastors Tayo and Bunmi Ojajuni and Gbenga and Bisi Adenuga

Dates: **May 14–17, 2020**
Name: Zonal Conference/Provincial Pastor's visit
Theme: **Emmanuel**
CANCELLED DUE TO COVID-19 PANDEMIC RESTRICTIONS

Dates: **May 21–22, 2021**
Name: Zonal Conference/Provincial Pastor's visit
CANCELLED DUE TO COVID-19 PANDEMIC RESTRICTIONS

Dates: **April 22–24, 2022**
Name: Zonal Workers' Conference/Provincial Pastor's visit
Theme: **The Fulfilled Minister**
Venue: Cornerstone Chapel Moncton (CCM)
Speakers: Pastors Olu and Oyin Ayeni and Gbenga and Bisi Adenuga

Dates: **May 18 - 21, 2023**
Name: Provincial Conference
Theme: **Beyond Expectations**
Venue: Mount Allison University (MtA) Sackville
Speakers: Pastors Ade and Grace Okonrende and Gbenga and Bisi Adenuga

Dates: **May 17–18, 2024**
Name: Provincial Conference/Continental Overseer's visit
Theme: **The Sovereign Lord**
Venue: Mount Allison University (MtA) Sackville
Speakers: Pastors Femi and Bukky Olawale and Gbenga and Bisi Adenuga

Dates: **June 16, 2024**
Name: Atlantic Canada Rally/General Overseer's visit
Theme: **Let There Be Light**
Venue: Mount Allison University (MtA) Sackville
Speakers: Pastor Enoch and Folu Adeboye

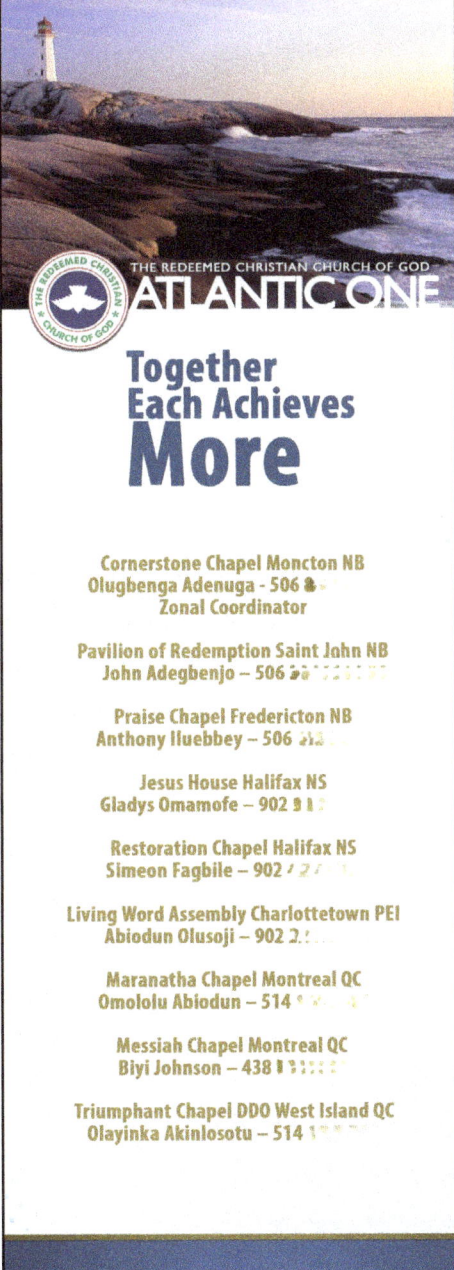

(2014) RCCG AT 1 Zonal Parishes Directory

2014 AT 1 Zonal Conference

(2014) AT 1 Zonal Conference Participants

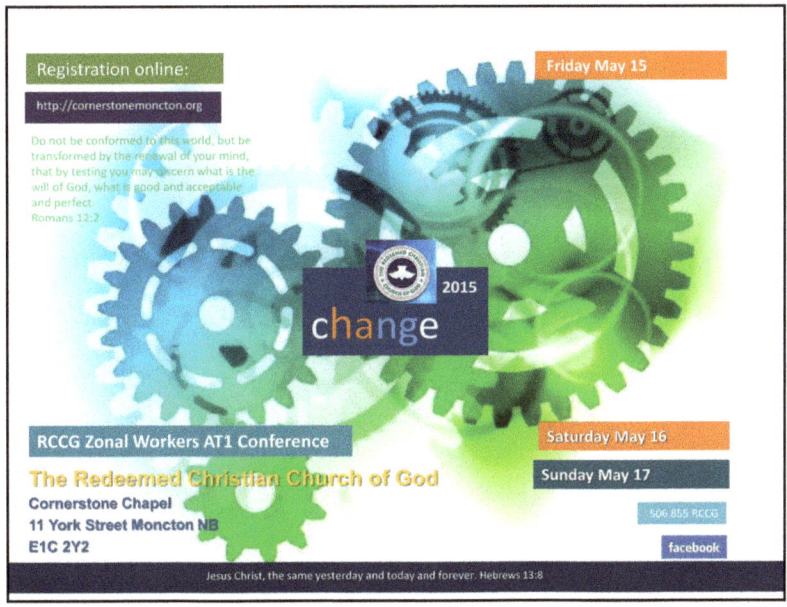

2015 AT 1 Zonal Conference

(2015) AT 1 Zonal Conference Participants

2016 AT 1 Zonal Conference

(2016) Pastor Toyin Dada and Pastor Bisi Adenuga at the AT 1 Zonal Conference

Pastor E.A. Adeboye
General Overseer

10830-96 Street Edmonton,
Alberta T5H 2I9, Canada
Tel: 1(780) 656-5917
Fax: 1(589) 400-9663

September 7, 2016

Pastor Gbenga Adenuga
Pastor@cornerstonemoncton.org

Live It Loud 2017

Dear Pastor Adenuga,

We, the Young Adult and Singles Ministry of RCCG Canada, are excited to officially let you know of our desire to hold our next Young Adults and Singles Conference, Live it Loud, in the city of Moncton. By God's inspiration, Our Theme this year is **"Greater Works", John 14:12**.

We write this letter to you, the zonal pastor for AT-1, to humbly request for your zone to accept us and host our conference in 2017. The conference holds from July 27-30, 2017 (the last weekend in July). We also trust that your zonal rep on our team, bro John Cuma, would be working closely with you as we engage in preparations towards the conference.

Sir, our brethren from AT-1 have been a great and consistent blessing to this ministry. Further, we have greatly appreciated the love and support you have shown us as zonal Pastor for AT-1. We are excited at the prospect of coming to fellowship in your home and we believe it will be a blessing to us all.

We look forward to your positive confirmation, an honor for us indeed. Kindly respond to us at our contact e-mail address - liveitloudya@gmail.com.

Thank you so much and God Bless you sir.

Yours in His Love,

Pst. Fatokun, Olumide Johnson
Young Adult & Singles Ministry of RCCG Canada
"Raising, Empowering for excellence... Be the example."

"Jesus Christ the same yesterday and today and forever." (Hebrews 13:8)
(The Redeemed Christian Church of God is a registered charity and donations are tax deductible)

Email: admin@rccgcanadayasm.org | Website: www.rccgcanadayasm.org

2017 Live It Loud (LIL) Conference

(2017) Live It Loud (LIL) Conference Speakers and Hosts

(2017) Excited Attendees at Live It Loud (LIL) Conference

2018 AT 1 Zonal Conference

2019 AT 1 Zonal Conference

(2019) AT 1 Zonal Conference Participants

(2019) AT 1 Zonal Conference Participants.
From Left: Pastors William and Dayo Onosesan;
Pastor Mrs. Bunmi Ojajuni, Co–Pastor in Charge of
Province; and Pastors Bunmi and Tunde Apantaku

(2019) AT 1 Zonal Conference Celebration

2023 AT 1 Provincial Conference

2024 AT 1 Provincial Conference

RADAH Magazine 2016 Fall Edition

RCCG ATLANTIC CANADA CONFERENCE PROFILE

RADAH Magazine 2016 Spring Edition

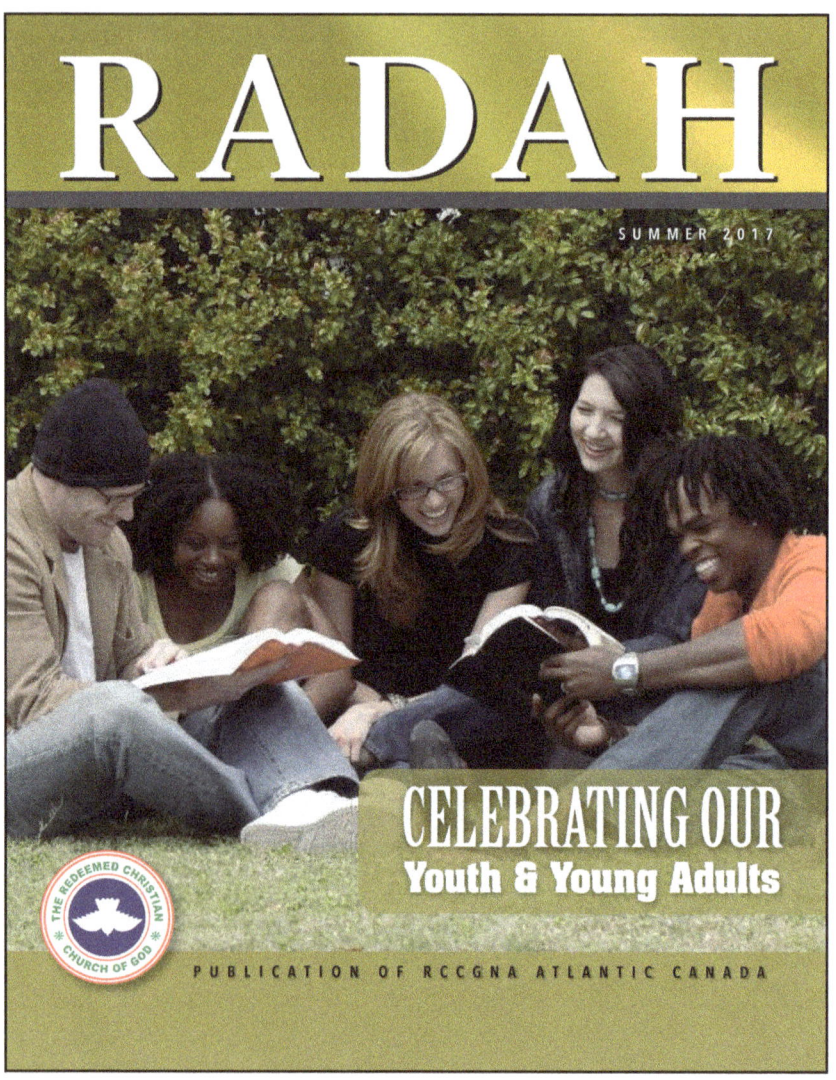

RADAH Magazine 2017 Summer Edition

RCCG ATLANTIC CANADA CONFERENCE PROFILE

RADAH Magazine 2018 Spring Edition

About the Compilers

Tunde Apantaku, MD, is an ordained minister in The Redeemed Christian Church of God North America (RCCGNA) and the officiating Assistant Pastor of Pavilion of Redemption Saint John NB, Canada. He is a practicing physician in pediatric psychiatry. He is also a teaching professor at Redeemer's University North America (formerly RCCGNA Seminary), and God is using him as a torch bearer to influence the next generation of change agents. He and his wife, Pastor Bunmi Apantaku, are blessed with three children (Nifemi, Subomi, and Tofunmi). He has written a number of books related to spirituality, including *The Depths of True Worship: Two Insights into Worshipping in Truth and in Spirit* (2023).

Gbenga Adenuga is the pastor-in-charge of Atlantic Canada (AT1) Province of The Redeemed Christian Church of God (RCCG) and the senior pastor of Cornerstone Chapel Moncton, NB, Canada. His primary focus is to equip people with the power of the word to pursue their purpose with the kind of passion and perseverance that he exemplifies.

www.ingramcontent.com/pod-product-compliance
Lightning Source LLC
Chambersburg PA
CBHW051549010526
44118CB00022B/2642